HowExpert Presents

# Paris 2.0

Top 101 Places to Visit in Paris to
Have Fun, Take Pictures, Meet
People, Eat Food, See Beautiful
Views, and Experience Paris France
to the Fullest From A to Z

# HowExpert with
# Caitlyn Knuth

## Copyright HowExpert™
## www.HowExpert.com

**For more tips related to this topic,
visit HowExpert.com/paris.**

# Recommended Resources

- HowExpert.com – Quick 'How To' Guides on All Topics from A to Z by Everyday Experts.
- HowExpert.com/free – Free HowExpert Email Newsletter.
- HowExpert.com/books – HowExpert Books
- HowExpert.com/courses – HowExpert Courses
- HowExpert.com/clothing – HowExpert Clothing
- HowExpert.com/membership – HowExpert Membership Site
- HowExpert.com/affiliates – HowExpert Affiliate Program
- HowExpert.com/writers – Write About Your #1 Passion/Knowledge/Expertise & Become a HowExpert Author.
- HowExpert.com/resources – Additional HowExpert Recommended Resources
- YouTube.com/HowExpert – Subscribe to HowExpert YouTube.
- Instagram.com/HowExpert – Follow HowExpert on Instagram.
- Facebook.com/HowExpert – Follow HowExpert on Facebook.

# Table of Contents

**Recommended Resources** .............................. 2

**Chapter 1: The World's Paris, Your City of Light** .............................................................. 8

*An Open Mind Leads to an Open City* .......................... 9

*A Few Things to Forget Before You Travel to Paris* ............ 11

**Chapter 2: Restaurants and Café Must-Stops: The Heart and Pride of Flavorful Paris** ......... 13

*For Fun and People Watching* ................................ 13

    La Terrasse du 7eme ...................................... 13

    Les Deux Magots ......................................... 14

    Le Rive Gauche .......................................... 15

    Au Cadet de Gascogne ..................................... 15

    Café Marly .............................................. 16

*For a Fabulous Taste of French Cuisine* ...................... 17

    Auberge Bressane ........................................ 17

    Pasco ................................................... 18

*For Feeling Fancy and Free* .................................. 18

    Café de la Paix ......................................... 18

*For Your Sweet Tooth* ........................................ 19

    Angelina ................................................ 20

*For Your Global Gastronomy Needs* ............................ 20

    Miyako .................................................. 21

    Anahuacalli ............................................. 21

    Samo .................................................... 22

    Buddha Bar .............................................. 22

    New Jawad ............................................... 23

*For a Taste of Home and a Cure for the Collector's Craving* 23

    Hard Rock Café Paris .................................... 23

*For your Finer Side, a Michelin Must-Try* .................... 24

    Epicure ................................................. 25

**Chapter 3: Historical Landmarks for History Buffs** ...................................................... 26

*Les Invalides and All Things Napoleon* ...................... 26

*École Militaire- Military Marvels in Modern Paris* .......... 27

*The Panthéon* ............................................... 28

*La Madeleine* ............................................... 29

*Obelisk of Luxor* ........................................... 29

*Parisian Boulevards-The Military Might of France* ........... 30

# Chapter 4: Places to Dine and Dance ........... 32

*Barrio Latino-A Haven of Tapas, Salsa and Tango*..............*32*
*Seine Side Tango Time*................................................................*33*
*Pub St. Michel For Club Lovers at Heart*.............................*33*
*Doobies for Bubbles and the Beat* ..........................................*34*

# Chapter 5: An Academic Angle on Paris........35

*La Sorbonne-An Historic Staple of Parisian Higher
Education* .....................................................................................*35*
*The American University of Paris-Where the World
Converges on Education*............................................................*36*

# Chapter 6: Major Museums not to Miss ....... 38

*Falling in Love with the Louvre* ..............................................*39*
*Passing a Modern Moment at The Pompidou Center* ...........*41*
*Rodin for the Romantic in All of Us* ......................................*42*
*Musée de Cluny-A look at Medieval Life in the Middle of
Modern Paris*..............................................................................*43*
*Musée d'Orsay: Visit When the Clock Strikes Now* ...............*44*

# Chapter 7: Off the Beaten Path Attractions .. 45

*Montmartre's Hidden Vineyard-Clos Montmartre*...............*45*
*Edith Piaf Museum-The Performance of a Lifetime* ..............*46*
*Le Refuge des Fondus-Dinner, Wine and a Baby Bottle Too* *47*
*Le Grand Musée du Parfum-A Scented Tour of Parisian
Perfume* .......................................................................................*47*
*A Walk Down Rue Cler* .............................................................*48*

# Chapter 8: Parisian Parks for All Ages and
Interests ...................................................... 50

*Jardin des Tuileries*...................................................................*50*
*Parc Monceau* ............................................................................ *51*
*Parc des Buttes Chaumont*....................................................... *51*
*Esplanade des Invalides* ...........................................................*52*
*Champs de Mars*.........................................................................*53*
*Jardin de Luxembourg* ..............................................................*54*

# Chapter 9: Exclusively for the Kids...............55

*Activities that Reach for the Sky-Tour Montparnasse*..........*55*
*Go-Kart at the Champs de Mars* ..............................................*56*
*Carousel at the Jardin de Luxembourg* ..................................*57*
*Jardin des Plantes: A Secret Garden for Kids of all Ages and
Imagination* ...............................................................................*58*
*Parc Astérix-Where Children Come Face-to-Face with
Medieval France*.........................................................................*58*
*Disneyland Paris-A Magical Destination* ...............................*59*

*Ferris Wheel Rides at the Place de la Concorde*..................*60*
*Time to Trampoline at Jardin des Tuileries*........................ *61*

## Chapter 10: Shopping Stops for the Fashion Lover ........ 62

*Les Halles*.................................................................*62*
*Bon Marché*...............................................................*63*
*Boulevard Saint Germain-des-Prés*...............................*64*
*Avenue Georges V*......................................................*64*
*Champs Élysées* .........................................................*65*
*Souvenir Central: Montmartre* .....................................*66*
*Clignancourt Flea Market-Les Puces*.............................*67*
*Les Cléfs d'Or Concierge and Shopping Service* ...............*68*

## Chapter 11: Hotels You Can't Miss .............. 70

*George V*....................................................................*70*
*Hotel La Comtesse* .................................................... *72*
*Hotel Eiffel Rive Gauche* ........................................... *73*
*Hotel Ritz Paris* ....................................................... *74*
*Shangri-La Paris* ...................................................... *75*

## Chapter 12: Places Famous for Those Whose Hearts Beat for Art........................................77

*Les Deux Magots* ...................................................... *77*
*Hotel d'Angleterre- Room 14* ..................................... *78*
*Picasso's Residence-Montmartre* ................................. *79*
*Giverny*.................................................................... *80*

## Chapter 13: Seine Side Excursions................81

*Walking Route from Towers to Spires* ......................... *81*
*Trocadéro Aquarium* .................................................*83*
*Bateaux Mouches River Cruise* ...................................*83*
*Rent it to Believe it-House Boats on the Seine* ...............*84*
*Bridges to Leave Footprints Over and Under*..................*85*

## Chapter 14: Theaters That Bring the Dramatic City to Life and Stage.................................... 88

*Palais Garnier* ..........................................................*88*
*Grand Rex*.................................................................*89*
*Cirque d'Hiver* ..........................................................*90*
*Crazy Horse* ............................................................. *91*
*Moulin Rouge* ...........................................................*92*
*Champs Élysées Theaters* ...........................................*93*

## Chapter 15: City Views Worth Finding ........ 94

*Montmartre- It's Time to Make the Climb* .....................*95*
*Trocadéro- A World Fair View of Past and Present*.............*96*

*Tour Montparnasse-A Bird's Eye View on Paris* .................. *97*
*Place de la Concorde and her Several Spectacular Views* ....*98*
*La Defense and the Grand Modern Arch* ..............................*100*
*Paris by Bike-The Value and View of Vélib* .......................... *101*

# Chapter 16: Cemeteries for Seeking the Sacred and Serene .................................................103
*Cimetière Montparnasse* .......................................*103*
*Cimetière Montmartre* .......................................*104*
*Père Lachaise* .......................................*105*
*The Catacombs of Paris* .......................................*106*
*Cimetière Passy* .......................................*107*

# Chapter 17: Castles, Kings and the Churches Between .................................................109
*Basilique de St. Denis* .......................................*109*
*Château de Vincennes* .......................................*110*
*Château de Fontainebleau* .......................................*111*
*Château de Versailles* .......................................*112*
*Basilique du Sacré-Coeur de Montmartre* .......................................*113*

# Chapter 18: The Must-See Major Monuments Before You Leave ..................................... 115
*The Eiffel Tower* .......................................*116*
*Arc de Triomphe* .......................................*118*
*Champs Élysées* .......................................*119*
*Cathédrale Notre-Dame de Paris* .......................................*120*
*La Conciergerie* .......................................*121*

# Chapter 19: Last Minute Tips and Tricks ....124
*Taking Control of the Tourist Ticket Situation* .................... *124*
*Making the Most of the Metro* .......................................*125*

# Chapter 20: À Bientôt- See You soon! ......... 127
# About the Expert .................................................130
# Recommended Resources ......................... 131

# Chapter 1: The World's Paris, Your City of Light

## The Eternal Inspiration of Paris for Travelers

We would like to think that travel is a choice, but ultimately, it's a calling. Some will choose to listen, and others may ignore it altogether, but the call is clear. At the core of humanity is a need to know the world we inhabit in a way nobody else has known it before. What is it about exploration that pushes us forward beyond logic or reason? Like a siren, the desire to travel calls us to try something that we've only dreamed of silently within the routine of our daily lives.

Destinations call to people for any number of reasons and deep-seated desires, but perhaps on the ever-growing list of cities known for bringing throngs of admirers to new boarders, Paris, France reigns supreme. The City of Light has a notorious reputation for pulling travelers in and never letting them go. Writers and artists, innovators and the curious at heart across genres, generations and centuries have become enamored with the city. Her effect on these individuals is evident in the proof they leave behind for others to find.

Hemingway, Stein and Wilde left it in ink on pages of novels attributed to the influence of the Parisian way of life. Picasso, Rodin and Monet left loving remnants of adoration through sculpture and paint. Still others in our modern era can't seem to get enough of what

Paris has to offer either. Endless films have been produced and continue to roll out as testimony to that certain *something* only the City of Love and Light seems to be able to provide her citizens and visitors alike. From *French Kiss* to *Midnight in Paris* and *Paris, Je t'aime,* modern fascination with the city can't help but find it's way onto the big screen where it continues to captivate.

The story of time itself proves that Paris is a place that belongs to the world, but the beauty of traveling to this mysteriously compelling city is that each experience is individual. Somewhere between the baguettes and rosé, the history, the charm and fashion is a place that feels as if it was meant for only you to discover. Somewhere along the Seine is a path and perhaps a particular moment, waiting for only *you* to experience. Paris calls incessantly for you to leave your footprints along the many boulevards, winding cobblestone streets and avenues that she hosts. The only question is whether or not you'll answer the call and come running after all.

## An Open Mind Leads to an Open City

Travel can be done in so many ways, but when it comes to traveling to Paris, an open mind is best. There are destinations on the map that require extensive planning in order to be experienced in the most effective way possible. There are places that demand order and strategy to be appreciated. Paris is not typically one of these cities. In fact, there is more to be gained from an attitude of appreciation than a regulated plan. For many travelers, this is counter intuitive, but the magic of Paris lies in the truth that the city is best experienced when one has a bullet point of must see stops perfectly aligned with a willingness to be open to any and every experience that might come your way unexpectedly.

There are of course, the big name mentions that should be attended to. The Mona Lisa, The Eiffel Towers and Notre Dame, just to name a few, call Paris home. However, if you are hoping to take something uniquely yours away from your French adventure, it's worth your time to allow the unexpected to happen on your way to these major sites, tastes and experiences. Paris is a city of beauty and intrigue as well as a city of savory secrets, if only you will listen.

Whether your heart lies with art, fashion, history, literature or food—Paris caters to the dreamer in all of us. Don't be surprised when on your way to that restaurant you've seen in every guidebook you've ever picked up, you discover one a bit more delicious on the side street you mistakenly took. Feel free to be stunned at the awe-inspiring view you stumble upon as you make your way to the Louvre. The art that is the city itself can inspire as much, if not more, than the famed works you'll make your way towards step by step. If you're looking to make the most of Paris, the best advice to take is to keep your strictly regimented expectations closed down, just for a while, and keep your mind and eyes very much open.

# A Few Things to Forget Before You Travel to Paris

We live in a world and time that is both powered and thrives on an impossibly high set of expectations. There is a tendency to unknowingly pack these preconceived notions and ideals with us, snuggly tucked into our minds and suitcases as we take off for new destinations. It might be based on something we heard from those who traveled there before us. It could be something we saw posted moments after it happened to someone else. It might be a vision of a new city that we've crafted in our minds that's come from the movies we've watched over and over again. Whatever it is, and whatever its origins, it's worth forgetting before you board the plane for Paris.

In general, the idea of France comes with a diverse array of assumptions. Seen under a variety of cultural lenses, Paris in particular, is attached to misguided ideas of difficulty and distain for tourists. Keep in mind that assumptions prior to travel have the ability to take away from an authentic experience. Do yourself a favor and drop these cliché expectations on the tarmac, simply get in your seat, buckle up and get ready to meet Paris for yourself. This time around, it's ok to forget a few things before you go.

You see, once those unfounded assumptions are very much gone, your experience in Paris can truly begin. While this guide will point out 101 places to see, things to do and tips to keep in mind to help start your trip, at the end of the day, it's exactly and only that—a guide. It is not written in stone and it's not meant to shape every moment of your time in the City of Light.

It is quite simply the first bullet point list you'll glance at and then fold up as you make your way down the street, open to your own adventure. My hope is that these select few destinations that span the topics of art, food, intellect and everything in between are mere starting points for what you will inevitably discover along the way.

Kindly treat this as a travel notebook to be added to over time. After all, the call to travel is best when it's contagious and if your side notes and scribbles on this guide someday inspire others to take a trip as well, we will all be a successful and an integral part of the Paris that belongs to both you and me. With that... here are my notes from me to you, on the City of Love and Light. Feel free to do with these as you please and never stop adding to them. There is always so much more to be written. Bon Voyage!

# Chapter 2: Restaurants and Café Must-Stops: The Heart and Pride of Flavorful Paris

## For Fun and People Watching

Paris is a city built on taste. Awe-inspiring flavors are found around nearly every corner of the city. However, equally as tantalizing can be the opportunity to people watch as you sip your way through the city's many restaurants and cafés. Here are just a few options for making the most of seeing who has decided to visit the City of Light alongside you. Cheers and santé!

### La Terrasse du 7eme

*2 Place de l'École Militaire, 75007 Paris, France*

Snuggled between Avenue de la Motte Piquet and Avenue Bosquet in one of the most infamous neighborhoods in Paris, this Eiffel Tower adjacent café in the 7th arrondissement is one of the best people-watching locales you'll come across in the city. Situated on a bustling, tree lined intersection with views of the impressive past and present military school, this particular location is not only scenic, but lively at all hours of the day and night.

Charming hotels dot the area as well which puts you right in the heart of tourism as it mixes seamlessly with daily Parisian routine. Have a glass of rosé at a quaint patio table with a quintessential view on the world. Try the Quiche Lorraine if you have a casual culinary moment to spare. If you're feeling a bit more exotic, the buttery escargot are available at all hours. Between a vibrant wrap around patio and a red, plush interior seating option, the only thing you'll really have to do is decide what offers up the best view to get ready and watch Parisian life go by in the most flavorful way possible.

## Les Deux Magots

*6 Place Saint Germain- des- Prés, 75006 Paris, France*

Moving into the 6th arrondissement of Paris is well worth your time if people watching is a favorite pastime. This is where you'll find an incredible combination of historical meaning alongside eccentric personalities and tasty treats as well. If you feel the need to write your way through your stop at Les Deux Magots, you won't be alone. Once upon a time, Ernest Hemingway and his equally impressive literary counterparts called this very café their own stomping grounds. Inspirational, quirky and timeless, Les Deux Magots has a sort of siren call amongst cafés. Take some time for a coffee and a bit of Parisian inspiration when you linger at this well-versed locale.

# Le Rive Gauche

*6 Place Saint-Michel, 75006 Paris, France*

There's something helplessly romantic about combining literature, caffeine and tourism into your travels. Le Rive Gauche is the perfect place to stop for a quick drink as you admire the stunning St. Michel Fountain just across the way. Complete with St. Michael himself with hands raised victoriously in front of a massive stone building and mythical water fountains adorning each side, it's hard not to feel you've arrived somewhere historically vibrant.

There's often live music happening fountain side for your listening pleasure, and artists tend to be fantastically diverse in their program choices. Equally as intriguing is the Gibert Jeune bookstore that sits just next door. A popular tourist destination, this café is sure to please the people watcher and literary junkie at heart. Finish off your glass and stroll over to the many walls lined with books just waiting to be perused.

# Au Cadet de Gascogne

*4 Place du Tertre, 75018 Paris, France*

High up in the hills of the 18th arrondissement, lies the artistic heart of Paris in the form of the mystical Place du Tertre. The café Au Cadet de Gascogne isn't known for it's outstanding cuisine, but it's absolutely the ideal place to grab a drink, sit back and watch the creative world of Paris at work in real time. Nestled within a square that's directly next door to the famed Basilica Sacré Coeur, there's an unmistakable energy in this place that can't be denied. It practically hums with life and creative possibilities.

Home to a sea of colorful portrait artists lined up with easels, parchment and brilliantly colored chalks, as well as shuttered apartments lined with flower boxes, you'll inevitably feel at one with the pulse of artistic potential as you settle in at this culinary location. The constant flow of tourism alongside the many artists that have found inspiration here and have called this area home over the past century leaves you with a touch of the past in a most brilliant present.

## Café Marly

*93 Rue de Rivoli, 75001 Paris, France*

While it may not be the most inexpensive stop along the way, who can resist the chance to drink and dine at the Louvre itself? Café Marly offers open air seating options that allow visitors to gaze out between grand white washed stone pillars upon the most famous museum in the world. You'll also have a first-class view on the highly contested glass pyramid that now graces the main plaza and acts as a visitor entrance to the Louvre. Once you've found your chair, simply sit back and watch citizens of the world flock to this historic art icon while you sip the afternoon away in artistic and leisurely style.

# For a Fabulous Taste of French Cuisine

If you find yourself more in the mood for a classy, French dining experience after all of the people watching and café crème the day has offered up—Paris has you covered. Here are a few locations that never disappoint and kick the fancy factor up a notch without breaking the bank.

## Auberge Bressane

*16 Avenue de la Motte-Picquet, 75007 Paris, France*

Paris is a city of eternal intrigue, but part of her gastronomical power lies in her ability to adjust to the changing times as well. You may find that the best restaurants in the city are staples to their respective neighborhoods while remaining fluid in their ability to accommodate a variety of changing tastes and styles.

Auberge Bressane does exactly this! With a menu that changes with the season, this location remains exciting and innovative while retaining an atmosphere of traditional French luxury and comfort. Plush seating, rustic art work and an endless wine list accompany seasonally diverse culinary options from meat to vegetables. Complete with a wait staff that is well versed in tasteful options and perfect wine pairings, you have endless resources for creating the perfect culinary experience. Don't skip the escargot starter for an authentic French treat for your palate!

## Pasco

### *74 boulevard de la Tour Maubourg, 75007 Paris, France*

While it may initially conjure up ideas of Italian delights, don't let the name fool you. Pasco is a charming and strictly French dining destination and its atmosphere leaves no question about it. Warm, welcoming and delightfully delicious, Pasco plays host to a variety of traditional French cuisine that boasts both in quality and quantity. Try any of the steak options on the menu and pair with an eggplant starter to get your taste buds going.

# For Feeling Fancy and Free

Sometimes you just need to ditch moderation and give yourself an extravagant Parisian-style boost. This café must-see and sip location will leave you feeling French to your very core.

## Café de la Paix

### *5 Place de l'Opéra, 75009 Paris, France*

Stepping into the Café de la Paix is a luxurious experience in and of itself. There's a reason tourists and patrons alike flock to this location. Graced with gold gilded ceilings and exquisite frescos wall to wall, a visit here is an opportunity to grace yourself with those finer things in life you didn't even know you were missing!

If that's not enough, the café sits within walking distance of the infamous Opéra-Garnier. If you don't have time for a full meal, make sure to treat yourself to a Kir Royale. The easy-to-spot green awning and delicate gold lettering make it easy to find as you exit metro stop Opéra. It's a stop worth making time for because after all, sipping on Cassis and Champagne never tasted as good as it does when you're casually hanging around the same place Oscar Wilde used to call a favorite.

# For Your Sweet Tooth

Chefs across Paris have the art of culinary delights figured out. There's something in the way they have perfected the experience of a meal that speaks to people across the planet and brings them flying to the city for a taste of excellence. But what about those more concerned with what comes after? Not to worry—those with an insatiable sweet tooth have a place in Paris as well. When your chocolate craving needs attending to, there's only one place to go in the City of Light.

# Angelina

*226 Rue de Rivoli, 75001 Paris, France*

From floor to ceiling, Angelina shines in over-the-top glitz and glam and the deserts she provides are no less fantastic. Shining unapologetically in décor of crystal, gold and silver, this is every diner's dessert heaven. Once seated, you need look no further than Angelina's famous hot chocolate to satisfy your sugary side.

Extra creamy and beyond indulgent, this luxurious chocolate treat can be paired with any of the other hundreds of savory concoctions Angelina provides on a delicious, daily basis. For an over the top experience in sugary satisfaction, try a Montblanc. Perfect to share for two, the gooey marzipan topping easily gives way to a crunchy center. Dessert enthusiasts will find themselves satisfied beyond compare when met face-to-face with the delicious post-dinner menu available at Angelina.

# For Your Global Gastronomy Needs

Paris has earned top bragging rights when it comes to the reputation of French cuisine, but as a global city, it also hosts an incredible number of restaurants providing delicious dishes from around the world. Here's a look at a few treats that take us on a tasty trip across the continents.

# Miyako

*121 Rue de l'Université, 75007 Paris, France*

Situated in the 7th arrondissement just off Rue de l'Université, Miyako serves up Japanese cuisine at it's finest. With a friendly, knowledgeable staff quick to offer up helpful culinary tips, this location is comfortable, soothing and succulent. The atmosphere is set on point with a surrounding of traditional Japanese décor and music. Whether you're craving vegetable tempura or a sushi boat for two, Miyako doesn't disappoint. Pair any menu item with a seasonal sake and your experience is sure to be complete.

# Anahuacalli

*30 Rue des Bernardins, 75005 Paris, France*

Comfortable, cozy and vibrant, Anahuacalli offers diners a sophisticated twist on casual Mexican dining. With bright yellow walls and terracotta tiles to set the dynamic scene, you'll be transported to a south of the boarder experience within moments of walking in. From tacos to beans and every spiced soup in between, Anahuacalli delivers up fresh, authentic Mexican fare. Don't skip their famous margarita to give your dining experience a tasteful kick!

# Samo

## *1 Rue du Champ de Mars, 75007 Paris, France*

For a culinary adventure that takes you the way of Korea, Samo in the 7th arrondissement is a must try. Off the beaten path of the major monuments this neighborhood hosts, this restaurant is worth finding for the variety of flavor alone. Presented as a family-style dining establishment, customers are treated to a colorful arrangement of spices, fresh vegetables and greens that when combined with seasoned meats, create an unforgettable Korean barbecue experience. Feel free to mix and match items off the menu as you build your own individualized ready to taste treat.

# Buddha Bar

## *8-12 Rue Boissy d'Anglas, 75008 Paris, France*

If upscale, international chic is what you seek, Buddha Bar Paris is the place to be. A unique mix of new age edge and old-world Zen, Buddha Bar offers up a deliciously dusky atmosphere and hosts a variety of cuisine and drink options that are infused with creativity. With a flair for the artistic and a bold sense of global music, you'll be entranced by the endless beat around you while sipping a Mai Tai and enjoying a spicy tuna tartare with unmistakable Hawaiian influences.

# New Jawad

*12 Avenue Rapp, 75007 Paris, France*

Offering up a dynamic menu that combines Indian and Pakistani favorites, New Jawad is bound to dazzle diners looking for something bold. From lamb curry to rice based classics, this locale has found the perfect, savory balance between traditional and innovative cuisine. Don't be surprised when your aperitif shows up in stunning shades of blue! Visually appealing and always savory, it's a culinary stop that's delicious, authentic and fun for the whole family!

# For a Taste of Home and a Cure for the Collector's Craving

You've been exploring Paris and all that's available for taste and tongue, but now you crave just a little bit of the familiar along the way. Understandable and easy to relate to, this famous stop will cater to your dietary desires and offer up a few souvenirs along the way.

## Hard Rock Café Paris

*14 Boulevard Montmartre, 75009 Paris, France*

What's life without a little rock-n-roll? Paris is no stranger to the compelling pull of classic music and known the world over, Hard Rock has carved out a place for itself in the City of Love. You'll find all your menu favorites here including sizzling fajitas and decadent cheese burgers, alongside a never-ending stream of musical favorites and oldies to please your sights and sounds while you dine.

Take time to look around at the musical marvels the location has collected and proudly displayed on nearly every inch of wall space. After you've indulged your taste buds, make sure to swing by the souvenir shop and pick up the proof that you've experienced and dined at Hard Rock Café Paris!

# For your Finer Side, a Michelin Must-Try

Variety is abundant when it comes to satisfying each and every taste a person could imagine bringing to Paris. That being said, the French, and Parisians in particular, have always upheld the highest standards in the culinary realm. While numerous restaurants work towards achieving culinary accolades, no reward is held in higher esteem than the Michelin star. Receiving Michelin status ensures a restaurant will thrive and sets chefs a platform above the rest on a global scale. If finances are not an issue and you're ready to jump into the world of exquisite fine dining, a Michelin restaurant is a must-try.

# Epicure

## *112 Rue du Faubourg Saint-Honoré, 75008 Paris, France*

Chef Eric Frechon is the renowned name and culinary mastermind behind this 3-star Michelin marvel proudly settled in the 8th arrondissement. An expert in combining the most luxurious flavors and working wonders with ingredients that delight such as black truffle and foie gras, Epicure is a work of art in and of itself. If you venture out to this fine-dining experience, be sure to come in your finest attire as well. It is requested that diners present themselves in business casual clothing at all times. You'll be glad you did as you bask in the sun-soaked garden patio during the summer, or the regal French floral décor of the main dining room during the colder seasons.

# Chapter 3: Historical Landmarks for History Buffs

Through a contemporary lens, Paris is a symbol of all things new and chic. It has earned a reputation as a city to look towards for influence and direction in fashion, food and overall style. There is a tendency to lean on Paris for support in approaching life with a certain *je ne sais quoi*. However, despite her very modern edge, Paris has a deep history behind her that makes her who she is today. The city has conquered the trials of centuries and has the stories to prove it. For the history buffs among us, Paris is the ideal place to be.

## Les Invalides and All Things Napoleon

*Place des Invalides, 75007 Paris, France*

Despite her demure appearance, the City of Light has a past seeped in military might. It would seem from the very beginning, humanity's tendency to try and conquer all we see didn't leave Paris unscathed. The era of Napoleon is one that is on the tip of nearly every Frenchman's tongue to this day. Bold and charismatic to the point of teetering on the edge of dramatic nearly always, Napoleon shaped a lot of what Paris is in the modern age. Leaving a trail of major monuments in his military wake, Napoleon not only forged concepts of law in France that stand today but made sure his name would not be forgotten well into the future.

Today, his bones are entombed at Les Invalides. The construction of this gold-domed marvel was begun in in 1670 under the order of Louis XIV. What started out as a military hospital was later transformed into the military museum and Napoleonic resting place it is now. Impressive by standards of both presentation and prestige, one could guess it's exactly the place Napoleon would have picked for himself. An aspiring global conqueror, Napoleon might be intrigued to know that today, Les Invalides has influence that crosses the Atlantic. Interestingly enough, the dome of the capital building in Des Moines, Iowa was modeled nearly exactly after this Parisian landmark.

# École Militaire- Military Marvels in Modern Paris

*21 place Joffre - 75007 Paris*

Some of the most impressive and stunningly beautiful works of architecture in Paris link up seamlessly with a military past and present we might not recognize at first glance. One of these structural wonders is École Militaire. As you wander up the green, pristine lawns of the Champ de Mars, it rises to meet you, sometimes surprisingly so as it's counterpart, the Eiffel Tower, tends to be a popular destination at the other end of this particular park.

This military school is both impressive in it's sheer size and intricate architectural design. It was commissioned to be built by Louis XV in the early 1750's. A legitimate maze of training facilities, the school is still a major training hub for French military to this very day. As you walk around, take some time to notice just how ideal the Champs de Mars green space would have been once upon a time for the massive military formations it hosted.

# The Panthéon

*Place du Panthéon, 75005 Paris, France*

Mention "Pantheon" in conversation and the majority will assume you are referencing the glories of Rome. The incredible and ancient architecture that Rome calls her own was more than enough to influence the French. Modeled after the famed Roman masterpiece, the Panthéon which graces the Latin Quarter of Paris offers up its own unique view on the city.

Tickets can be purchased for a general tour of the church turned mausoleum, but a separate ticket can also be purchased to climb the dome itself. While the trek may require a few extra steps, it's worth the view. The Panthéon is a unique blend of the religious and secular as it continues to thrive in its own transition. Originally constructed by Jacques Germain-Soufflot as an homage to St. Geneviève, this massive construction now houses the remains of famed Frenchmen Voltaire and Rousseau. Today, it is more a dedication to the French story than a church at all.

# La Madeleine

*Place de la Madeleine, 75008 Paris, France*

If you're visiting the 8th arrondissement, it's hard to miss La Madeleine. With a metro stop dedicated to the same name, this landmark is easy to find and inevitably hard to forget. This striking work of architecture built in the style of a Roman temple was originally constructed to honor the military success of Napoleon. Today, it is a Roman Catholic church, but the unique fusion of it's military and religious roots is still evident.

Between massive, stone columns that line its looming façade, visitors enter only to find golden gilding and works of art that make one think of nothing other than the renaissance. The alter is dedicated to Mary Magdalene while frescos high above your head tell the story of Christianity featuring Napoleon. It's a unique blending of histories that comes together in the most impressive way.

# Obelisk of Luxor

*Place de la Concorde, 75008 Paris, France*

Arriving at the Place de la Concorde, one might mistakenly believe they have arrived in Egypt and you wouldn't be entirely wrong in your assumptions. Rising 75-feet into the air is the Obelisk of Luxor—a hieroglyphic- saturated statue gifted to the French in 1833. Over 3,000 years old and capped in gold, the obelisk once graced the entrance to the Temple of

Luxor in Egypt. It's gifting was a sign of comradery between the two nations and today, still represents France's interest in exploration and cultural preservation.

As with so many historical landmarks in Paris, the Obelisk of Luxor stands in stark contrast to the modern sites it coincides with. From the bustling hub of commerce which is the Champs Élysées, the Obelisk is completely visible. A perfect merging of ancient and modern, this is a must-see for those who love the places where timelines come to life and collide.

# Parisian Boulevards-The Military Might of France

Discovering and exploring Paris today is often an exercise in finding your way down winding, cobblestone streets. Narrow paths that lead to corner cafés are common, and off-the-beaten-path stone staircases to charming locales are not unheard of. However, equally as common are the grand boulevards you're sure to encounter. Turn an impossibly tiny corner only to find yourself on a bustling boulevard— lively with pedestrians and traffic.

It's worth your time to note that this was a purposeful plan put into place between 1850-1870. The credit for this complete reconstruction of Parisian logistics goes to Georges Haussmann. Some of the most notable grand boulevards today include Boulevard Haussmann, Boulevard St. Germaine and Rue du Rivoli, just to name a few. Their significance lies not only in the fact that their construction transformed the face of Paris from a maze of dark and dingy alleyways to massive roads ready to handle transportation, but also gave the city a military edge it didn't previously possess.

These new wide-open spaces made it possible for large displays of military force to parade down the street unhindered. Military equipment could be transported without damaging infrastructure and the French could observe the military might of their country on full display. Equally important was how the new concept of Parisian boulevards easily connected the city by creating central axis lines between banks where before there was clear separation. New levels of access, connectivity and openness gave Parisians a redefined perspective on their ability to move throughout their own city that was previously lacking.

As you walk down these boulevards yourself today, make sure to take a moment to imagine the military statements they were constructed to convey. Similarly, it's important to keep in mind that anytime dramatic change happens in history, there are consequences on both sides of the story. For all of the mobility that was gained, Haussmann's restructuring also put thousands of Parisians out of home and on the streets as neighborhoods were methodically torn down in the name of innovation. As your feet connect with history itself, take time to remember the many years of planning and preparation it took to make a vision reality. Take a moment to reflect on the many lives affected as these boulevards came into existence.

# Chapter 4: Places to Dine and Dance

## Barrio Latino-A Haven of Tapas, Salsa and Tango

*46 Rue du Faubourg St. Antoine, 75012 Paris, France*

When the desire to dance calls, Barrio Latino is there to answer. Walking in, you can't help but feel like royalty. From the plush red and gold couches to the grand staircase that connects four massive floors, Barrio Latino is a virtual stage no matter where you twirl.

Gilded lighting and dramatic, wrought iron twisted tables are the ideal stop if you're there to dine on tapas. When dinner's over, it's Salsa all around. While they do throw in a little Electronic and Reggae from time to time, Salsa is king in the Barrio. If you're new to the style, there are plenty of regulars on hand ready to help lead the way!

This location also offers up Tango lessons, generally on the weekends, if you're looking for something a bit more structured. Make sure to swing by and see what's on the schedule for the week and don't forget to bring your dance shoes with you!

# Seine Side Tango Time

_Quai Saint Bernard, Paris 75005, France_

Whether you're a novice, or part of the top Tango elite, there is a place for you on the Quai Saint Bernard. When the summer is hot, dancers of all levels make their way to this Seine-side locale daily to test their toes in the open air.

Once evening lessons have wrapped up for beginners, the ground is completely yours for the taking. Feel free to mix, mingle and dance the night away under the stars of Paris. Don't be surprised when those romantic notions you've secretly held onto come to life as they have a way of doing when it's summer in the heart of France.

# Pub St. Michel For Club Lovers at Heart

_19 Quai St Michel, 75005 Paris, France_

While not technically a club at heart, this pub/bistro by day tends to transform from eatery to beat-based dance floor when the night rolls around. Hosting two floors connected by a winding staircase, Pub St. Michel is located near the bustling Place St. Michel and looks out over the rolling Seine.

Scenic and delicious, this location is a great stop for a combination of drinks and dancing. Feel free to try one of their candy-garnished cocktails and make your way upstairs. The music tends to be heavy pop and if you're lucky, you might just show up on a night when they get the fog machine kick started!

# Doobies for Bubbles and the Beat

*2 Rue Robert Estienne, 75008 Paris, France*

This traditional French dining locale nestled just off of the Champs Élysées looks unassuming from the outside. Local residents know better. Stop in for lunch or dinner and you'll be met with an array of colorful, savory French dishes to satisfy your cravings. Sunday brunch is also a delicious must-try. Once the moon rises however, things change quickly at Doobies.

Complete with a live DJ, the entire restaurant transforms into a dance party. Tables are scooted to the far sides of the establishment and the floor is opened up to host your finest moves. With everything from pop, to electronic and Latin beats, Doobie's leaves no musical stone unturned. The bar is equally up for grabs as bartenders encourage the bravest of the bunch to make their way to new dance heights! Make sure to check in on ladies' night specials. Thursday night tends to be your best bet when looking for a free glass of champagne to accompany your killer moves.

# Chapter 5: An Academic Angle on Paris

While writers and artists have notoriously flocked to Paris in search of inspiration and beauty, there is an undeniable academic force that pulls those seeking the heights of higher education to the city as well. Across all educational fields, those aspiring to new levels of cerebral knowledge have looked to Paris as a source of learning. It's a place they come when they are seeking an opportunity to push knowledge to new limits and experiencing education at it's finest and most innovative.

## La Sorbonne-An Historic Staple of Parisian Higher Education

*47 rue des Écoles - 75005 Paris*

The heart and soul of global education lies in the Latin Quarter of Paris. Once upon a time, the infamous University of Paris called this neighborhood home. Today, La Sorbonne is the crown jewel of the academic world. Peppered with higher education institutions and universities, this area of Paris in particular has a heart that beats for higher learning and opportunity.

La Sorbonne calls to academics the world over both for its incredible history and opportunity. Built on medieval ruins of a university first built in the 13th century, La Sorbonne has dug its roots firmly on the past with a vision that is exclusively forward-thinking. Specializing in programs that span literature, social sciences and languages the university is not only physically massive, but largely diverse in what it offers up subject-wise to students.

There's something about walking in the footsteps of academics such as Marie Curie or Roland Barthes that makes all things seem possible when you're here. With an attitude of open thinking and a focus on creating global citizens, La Sorbonne is not only impressive and beautiful to wander by but delivers up a stunningly impressive list of alumni as well.

# The American University of Paris-Where the World Converges on Education

*6, rue du Colonel Combes, Paris 75007*

A full higher education experience abroad is not often first on the list when high school graduates sit down and contemplate colleges and universities to attend, but maybe it should be. The American University of Paris offers up a unique opportunity for students to not only achieve an education at a U.S. accredited institution, but to do so in the heart of European culture and life.

The idea is simple: Send students abroad long term and watch them return home one day with the ability to work and live with a dynamic global perspective. It was this idea that launched AUP in 1962 and continues to allow it to thrive today. Representing over 108 nationalities on it's city-based campus, The American University of Paris offers degree programs spanning Global Communications, Journalism, Business and International Relations.

While the majority of classes are instructed in English, there is a French requirement that ensures students leave their program, either undergraduate or graduate, with an ability to communicate fluidly in French. With campus squarely set in the middle of the 7th arrondissement, the university is easy to find and inspiring in its proximity to major Parisian icons such as the Eiffel Tower.

Feel free to stop by the main office during your visit as school officials and student volunteers are happy to give impromptu tours. Just for a while, you can experience higher education as a completely immersive experience in Paris.

# Chapter 6: Major Museums not to Miss

If the many restaurants in Paris are renowned for their ever-changing taste and style, the same could be said for the infamous museums that grace nearly every inch of the city. This may seem counter intuitive at first, but at second glance, it would make sense that the most historically relevant locations in Paris, whether tucked into discreet corners or boldly obvious landmarks, are also those that have been flexible enough to endure the tests of time.

This alone marks them as the most adaptable to an ever-changing world. The museums of Paris are plentiful, but there are a few not to be missed. While all museums house what is important about the art of past and present, there are some that hold a history so vivid and valuable it would be shameful to pass by without stopping in. There is something that happens when you walk into a museum in Paris—you are met by not only the Paris that was, but the Paris that is, and your presence there only adds to the atmosphere.

Some say that museums are the homes of all that is antique, but this just can't be all there is to it. Yes, museums house stories of yesterday, but they are also charged with the responsibility of bringing life to all that is beautiful and creative and worth noticing in today's world as well. They are a testament to where we have been, and a hope for where we are going. Here are a few fantastic starting points where history and modernity find their delicate balance.

# Falling in Love with the Louvre

*Rue de Rivoli, 75001 Paris, France*

Perhaps the most historically relevant and adaptable of all the museums in Paris continues to be the Louvre. Known as the home of countless stunning and meaningful works of art, it's hard to separate a trip to this massive museum without associating it with Leonardo da Vinci's Mona Lisa. Venus de Milo ranks up there on the must-see list alongside the Winged Victory of Samothrace that stands proudly on the top of a grand staircase. Split into three major wings including Denon, Sully and Richelieu, it would be a supernatural feat to see all there is to see within the span of a day. In fact, it's estimated that if you spent a mere 30 seconds at each work of art, it would still take you around 100 days to see it all.

For this reason, there are two ways to approach the Louvre. The first is to have a few priceless works picked out ahead of time so you have a plan of action when you reach the entrance. The Denon wing takes you directly to the big-name painters and sculptors you've probably got in mind today and could be a smart starting point. The main entrance to the Louvre winds down through the central glass pyramid but tends to host an endless line of visitors the majority of the time. Instead, try the Portes des Lions for a faster entrance on most days. The literal translation is *Lions Door*, and for this very reason it's hard to miss because as promised, the doors lie between statues of those very felines.

The other option is to take the completely opposite approach to your visit. Pick an amount of time you want to stay and simply observe, wander and let the Louvre do its magic for you. While it's incredible to witness those artful works we've heard and learned about over the years, there are endless opportunities for inspiration along the way that are more unexpected than anything else. The halls of the Louvre are covered in impressive and sometimes lesser known works that tend to speak to visitors in mysterious ways. Endlessly colorful and captivating, it can be exciting to let art speak to you in a more personal and profound fashion.

Once you've discovered the Louvre's interior, don't forget to enjoy what's outdoors as well, because it's equally impressive. The Louvre has a detailed and complex past and the effects of it's changing status are evident in it's very architecture. With roots dating back to 1190, the museum has transformed over time from city fortress to residence for royalty and finally, the museum it is today. Take time to walk the central courtyard where the modern glass pyramid contrasts starkly against the detailed stone work that graces the majority of the façade. Gently cascading fountains surround the pyramid and can be a scenic place to rest your feet and people watch for a while. Turning towards the Tuileries Gardens gives you an amazing view down towards the Place de La Concorde. It's in fact, hard to find a direction that doesn't inspire on some level, so make sure you don't miss the chance to see it for yourself.

# Passing a Modern Moment at The Pompidou Center

*Place Georges-Pompidou, 75004 Paris, France*

On the opposite end of the artistic spectrum, the Centre Georges Pompidou caters explicitly to the modern art movement. If you wander through the 4th arrondissement, it's hard to miss. Unique in style and unapologetically a statement on innovation, the museum and it's jagged, steel-based architecture and outer stairwell designed as colorful tubing demand to be acknowledged.

The purpose of this modern art museum is two-fold. The interior is rather open compared to standard museum layouts and is meant to be viewed as both a modern gallery as well as public space. Curators encourage public works and events to be held at the museum as much as they encourage patrons of the arts to come to enjoy what's on display. The space is unique in that it also houses a public library and a research center for the arts.

Admirers of artists such as Andy Warhol, Mark Rothko and Jackson Pollock can be sure to be inspired by the opportunity to be in such close proximity to works that question and challenge artistic convention.

# Rodin for the Romantic in All of Us

## *77 Rue de Varenne, 75007 Paris, France*

Rodin is a household name in the art world, and to this day, remains one of the most provocative sculptors in his ability to evoke emotion, passion and a longing for love. With an exceptional talent for bringing a single moment to life in stone, Rodin left an array of works in Paris that speak to our heads and hearts in equal parts.

Splendid creations crafted chiseled from rock such as *The Thinker* or *The Kiss* have an innate ability to make observers step back and marvel at the precision required to make marble appear fluid. There is something about Rodin's ability to carve an intimate moment into history that speaks to a craft ahead of his time.

If you're looking to experience Rodin's works up close while wandering in his very footsteps, Musée Rodin is a must-see. Divided between the hotel he used as a workspace and his personal home, this museum feels like the perfect mix between gorgeous gallery and intimate home tour. His personal collection of art is still on display alongside his own creations, giving the entire tour a feeling of personal authenticity.

Once you've stepped into each and every room, make your way out to the lush, colorful garden. It's here that you might feel most connected to Rodin. Scattered throughout the garden are an array of sculptures. Romantic and impressive, this space will leave you feeling you've encountered Rodin both as an artist and a man who once called Paris home.

## Musée de Cluny-A look at Medieval Life in the Middle of Modern Paris

*6 Place Paul Painlevé, 75005 Paris, France*

With a history reaching back all the way to the 1300's, the Musée de Cluny is your first stop when you're craving an immersive experience of medieval art in the heart of Paris. From the outside, the museum is a stunning mix of renaissance and gothic architecture— a testament to it's centuries of transformation. Once inside, the ancient scene is set with an incredible display of everything from stained glass windows to illuminated manuscripts and sculpture.

Perhaps the most notable display comes in the form of the famed medieval tapestries the museum houses. The most renowned include *The Lady* and *The Unicorn*. Impressive in their sheer size, detail and immaculate preservation, these works of hand and art are worth your time to experience.

Make sure to make your way to the exterior of the museum once you've had your fill of exquisite woven wonders to take in the remnants of the Roman thermal baths that still remain semi-intact to this day.

# Musée d'Orsay: Visit When the Clock Strikes Now

*1 Rue de la Légion d'Honneur, 75007 Paris, France*

Musée d'Orsay's ability to keep up with the changing times comes in the unique form of its grand transition from 20th century train station to the famed museum that it is today! Easily identifiable by the massive façade-front clocks it hosts on the Seine's left bank, Musée d'Orsay opened its doors as the premiere location for witnessing all that is impressionism in 1986.

Open, airy and filled with just the right light, Musée d'Orsay gives visitors the opportunity to mix and mingle with those who made impressionism a staple in the world of art including Monet, Renoir, Degas, Van Gogh and Cezanne just to name a few. Additionally, the museum highlights French art from the 20th century and includes a wing dedicated to photography.

While the façade of this museum is beautiful to encounter from the outside, it comes with a delicious treat as well if you visit from the interior. The backside of the massive clock is the central décor piece of the museum's main café. Feel free to sit and have a leisurely coffee literally, behind time itself. For an even more impressive vantage point, saunter out the cafés side doors for a beautiful balcony view of of Paris below.

# Chapter 7: Off the Beaten Path Attractions

There's something about the unknown that calls to all of us. While it can be comforting to know that your guidebook can give you the lay of the land, some of the best gems of Paris are hidden off the standard route. They take a bit longer to find, but when you stumble upon a lesser known highlight, the city comes to light in a way you might never have expected. From magical to musical, here are a few hideaways that are worth discovering!

## Montmartre's Hidden Vineyard- Clos Montmartre

*Rue des Saules, 75018 Paris, France*

The gravitational pull of all things artistic will inevitably pull you to Montmartre. Lively, musical and endlessly impressive in architecture, this hilltop scene draws tourists from around the globe. Once you've had your portrait drawn free hand and visited the stunning Sacré Coeur, there's a lesser known locale that should be on your must-see list.

You might be surprised to find a thriving vineyard right in the heart of Paris. This jewel of a secret is tucked away just behind the famous Place du Tertre on Rue des Saules. Owned and operated by the city of Paris, this vineyard's profits get turned around into project funds that exclusively serve the 18th arrondissement. Serene and unique in it's ability to continue to forge a green path in core of the city, you'll recognize wines that are produced from this pristine urban plot by their *Clos Montmartre* label.


# Edith Piaf Museum-The Performance of a Lifetime

*5 Rue Crespin du Gast, 75011 Paris, France*

There is music that rings true internationally as identifiably and quintessentially French. Above all, *La Vie en Rose* is often turned to as an anthem of French Culture and creative past. It has captivated audiences for decades, largely due to it's famous vocalist, Edith Piaf. If you're in the 11th arrondissement, don't miss the opportunity to explore Edith's former apartment turned museum for an intimate look into the chanteuse's life.

Open by appointment only, this museum offers free admission accompanied by a priceless experience. With exceptional displays of books, painting and personal items the artist held dear, you can't help but feel that life is a bit rosier all around after this off-the-path excursion.

# Le Refuge des Fondus-Dinner, Wine and a Baby Bottle Too

*17 Rue des Trois Frères, 75018 Paris, France*

You expect high class to meet you gracefully at the door when you set foot in Paris. For the most part this is absolutely the case, which makes this stop an off the beaten path must try. Leave your expectations far behind as you step into this cozy restaurant near Montmartre. Get close and comfortable with your dearest travel buddies as you dine on delectable fondue and laugh the night away shoulder-to-shoulder around charming wooden tables.

What makes this place the most memorable is by far the wine experience. While it might not be the city's finest fare, it is absolutely the most memorable! Served in baby bottles, (you read that right), it will be an *expérience du vin* like you've never had before. Come in with an appetite and an appreciation for all things fun and care free to make the most of your time.

# Le Grand Musée du Parfum-A Scented Tour of Parisian Perfume

*73 Rue du Faubourg Saint-Honoré, 75008 Paris, France*

Our five senses combined make for a powerhouse of daily experience. It's how we take in the world around us and how we perceive every situation we come across. However, of all our senses it may be scent that lingers longest. A certain smell can take us back to a specific day in childhood. A scent unexpected can propel us back to memories of those we loved. Scent is a powerful sense and Le Grand Musée du Parfum is dedicated entirely to the art of scent design.

Luxury brands and big names have long been associated with the art of perfume and Paris has its roots deeply embedded in the business. This fantastically modern museum takes time to look back at how that process developed while giving visitors the chance to immerse themselves in the sensations scent provides for as well. Get ready to not only learn how scent is harnessed into a tangible item for sale, but to experience scent on an entirely new level along the way.

# A Walk Down Rue Cler

### *Rue Cler, 75007 Paris, France*

Paris is made for walking and often, the best discoveries come when you choose to simply wander. If you're in the mood for browsing leisurely along and letting Paris happen as it will, start with Rue Cler in the 7th arrondissement. What could be described as a small market street can turn into a discovery all its own if you take the time to pass through. Colorful, flavorful and full of options, Rue Cler has a little something for everyone and a lot of personality in between.

There are several cafés lining the cobblestone walk of this street to sit and simply watch the world pass you by if you so choose. If you're searching for something a bit more active, take some time to check out the diverse array of items for sale in specialty stores from one end of this quaint street to the other. Shops offer up nearly everything including flowers, fish, oils, tea, gelato, cheese and of course, chocolate! Your taste buds will be tingling, and time simply flies when you step onto Rue Cler.

# Chapter 8: Parisian Parks for All Ages and Interests

## Jardin des Tuileries

### *113 Rue de Rivoli, 75001 Paris, France*

The Jardin des Tuileries may be massive, but it's one of those green spaces that somehow still feels manageable and personal. For this reason, it's an incredible stop whether you're a solo traveler or making your way through Paris with the entire family. The park is made up of tree lined walk ways that hug graveled paths. All around, you'll notice the luscious space is dotted with small cafés, shiny green benches and pristine ponds where lingering visitors mingle. This is the garden that majestically and famously fills the space between the Place de la Concorde and the Louvre.

In the summer months, the garden hosts a massive festival, but in all the best weather, you won't be hard pressed to find something to satisfy your sweet tooth. Small candy carts located throughout the garden will help curb your ice cream or cotton candy craving. Once you've found what you're looking for the options are endless as to how to fill time. Feel free to wander the paths leisurely or take a more stationary approach and soak up the sun next to one of the garden's two beautiful ponds. If you're lucky, you might come across some surprising artwork that tends to show up unexpectedly in the Tuileries and remains for nothing more than a fleeting moment—often placed with passion by local artists.

# Parc Monceau

*35 boulevard de Courcelles, 75008 Paris, France*

The 8th arrondissement is just the place to go if you're looking for a stop that lets you relax with a little romance on the side. Stunning, spacious and lush, Parc Monceau is a jewel in the heart of the neighborhood it calls home. Since it's construction under the command of the Dukes of Chartres in the 17th century, it's been admired and specifically sought out for its beauty. One of the park's most defining features is the intricate stonework that you stumble across as you explore it's many winding paths.

Perfect for biking, running or walking, this maze of pathways is also an exceptional location for wistful walks. From stone archways to statues and delicate bridges overlooking colorful gardens, you might find you fall in love as you go. Open green spaces give you the time to sit and simply watch the world pass you by if you prefer. Spending a few hours at Parc Monceau has an almost magical way of leaving you feeling both rested and simultaneously reinvigorated by the beauty that surrounds you.

# Parc des Buttes Chaumont

*1 Rue Botzaris, 75019 Paris, France*

While it may be a bit out of the way, a trek to the 19th arrondissement is worth your while if you're looking for a park with something a little different, and a stunning view or two. Impressive in both size and stature, Parc des Buttes Chaumont is a labyrinth of green spaces perfectly designed to impress. Rolling up and over hills, Parisians and tourists alike flock to this outdoor oasis to not only people watch, but city watch as well.

With unobstructed views of the city skyline, this park has an incredible ability to be an afternoon hideaway as well as a place that allows you to feel you are completely connected with the City of Light. Complete with an artistic mix of trees and greenery, the park draws a multitude of beautiful birds which brings professional and amateur bird watchers running. You'll want to take time to be impressed by the bridges, waterfalls and even caves to which this park plays host.

# Esplanade des Invalides

*1 Rue Fabert, 75007 Paris, France*

Just between the golden Pont Alexandre III and the glittering dome of Les Invalides lies a giant green space referred to as Esplanade des Invalides in the 7th arrondissement. While this isn't the park space to come to if you are looking for a quiet afternoon hidden away from the world, it is the ideal place to come if sun, socializing and soccer are top of mind.

Snuggled between bustling streets, Esplanade des Invalides is a wide-open lawn where you can sit under the sun with friends or jump into one of several pickup soccer matches that are going on during any given day. With spacious views and enough activity to fill your entire day, this is a lively hang out where you can come to mix and mingle the Parisian way.

# Champs de Mars

## 2 Allée Adrienne Lecouvreur, 75007 Paris, France

If it's green space with a view you're looking for, the Champs de Mars is a must see in the 7th arrondissement. Just around the corner from Esplanade des Invalides and placed pristinely between École Militaire and the looming Eiffel Tower, this park space was built for admiration. Simply settle in on one of the many benches along the gravel paths leading up to the glittering tower for an incredible view and even better people watching opportunity.

Not only is this the perfect place for that infamous tower-front picture, but if you're a runner, it's an incredible park to join Parisian joggers as they loop around rectangular pathways. Restructured for the 1900's World's Fair, the Champs de Mars offers up a postcard-worthy view through the tower to the hilltop Trocadéro just on the other side of the Seine.

# Jardin de Luxembourg

*Rue de Médicis - Rue de Vaugirard, 75006 Paris, France*

Rich in regality and hosting an endless line up of entertainment and art exhibitions for the public, the Jardin de Luxembourg should be the first stop when you're looking for that park that plays into your cultural cravings. Not known for being minimalistic, the Medici family, and more specifically, Queen Marie commanded the park's creation in 1612 and it's graced the 6th arrondissement ever since.

Today, it's a place to come and witness an incredible array of gardening feats. Filled with lush greenery and even more colorful floral combinations, you'll have the opportunity to wander and wonder between both the French and English gardens this park hosts. From roses to orchids and the many apple trees in between, it's something of a fantasy land come to life. Italian Baroque at heart but French in it's soul, the Jardin de Luxembourg is complete with an impressive palace, fountain, pond and stunning statues of France's most notable queens and royalty to finish off the exquisite experience.

# Chapter 9: Exclusively for the Kids

## Activities that Reach for the Sky-Tour Montparnasse

*33 Avenue du Maine, 75015 Paris, France*

At the very top of the tallest building in Paris, there's an opportunity to climb, or in this case, jump even higher. The Tour Montparnasse stands out as a looming presence in Paris as it reaches 59 floors into the sky. It's hard to miss on the Parisian skyline, so you can imagine how thrilling it will be for the kids to not only visit this cloud-side stop, but to take some time to see what unique activity *du jour* is being hosted for them at it's summit!

Top Jump Paris opened at the top of the tower in December 2017 as a series of open air trampolines that kids could come and bounce on 59 floors up and became an instant success with Parisians and tourists alike. Most recently, the trampolines have been replaced with massive plastic ball pits where visitors can jump in and play for 12 minutes of fun. These family friendly adventures rotate often and are worth experiencing just for the thrill of it. While these activities are primarily reserved for warm weather months and major holidays, they're a fun, unique and scenic way to see Paris and keep the kids (and maybe even the adults) entertained at the same time.

What's more, the Montparnasse tower tends to be far less crowded than other Paris hot spots, so if you buy your tickets online in advance, you'll have an easy time getting up to the top of the tower where the fun really begins!

# Go-Kart at the Champs de Mars

*2 Allée Adrienne Lecouvreur, 75007 Paris, France*

While throngs of tourists clamor for the chance to capture that perfect picture in front of the Eiffel Tower, those with little ones will be thrilled to hear that just in front of École Militaire is a picture perfect, lesser known playground that Parisian children love to frequent. Perhaps the most intriguing part of this play setup is the miniature Go-Kart track that is available during the summer months for just a few euro per ride.

Aimed at children between the ages of 2-5, this miniature track lets parents either push toddlers around the circle by hand, or wave from the sidelines as older kids peddle their way around. Not to worry, if you're traveling with a variety of ages and interests, there is a jungle gym and carousel just across the way that caters to kids with a little more need for speed. There's even a basketball court nearby for your teenagers who want to join a pickup game with locals and polish up on their French sports vocabulary while they're at it. Don't forget to stop by the ice cream carts that dot this area when you're done to celebrate your fun, family friendly find.

# Carousel at the Jardin de Luxembourg

*Rue de Médicis - Rue de Vaugirard, 75006 Paris, France*

Adults will be enthralled by the intricate beauty of Jardin de Luxembourg, but when it comes to the kids, let the past do the talking. A 19th century-built carousel still captivates children of all ages in this luscious park. Not only does it keep the entertainment level high but even kicks it up another notch by offering the opportunity for kids to play capture the ring while they ride. The game involves children holding a miniature lance in hand and aiming for small brass rings held by the carousel attendant to catch as they twirl by.

When your little ones have had their fill of the carousel, take a turn on the remote- control boats that are available in the garden's central pond. From capturing rings to controlling the fate of water-born toys, kids will find endless opportunities for fun and imagination to thrive in the heart of this exquisite garden.

# Jardin des Plantes: A Secret Garden for Kids of all Ages and Imagination

*57 Rue Cuvier, 75005 Paris, France*

While technically titled a *garden*, the Jardin des Plantes is both an incredible botanical center and natural history museum telling the tale and history of medicinal solutions over the many centuries in France. Opened to the public in 1640, this location in the 5th arrondissement continues to capture the imaginations of adults and children alike.

More often than not you'll stumble across an exotic exhibition on nature's most fascinating creatures as you wander through floral pathways outdoors, and incredible displays indoors as well. The Jardin des Plantes is the perfect place to bring children in Paris when you're looking for a location that is impressive, has space to explore nature alongside innovation, and is educational along the way.

# Parc Astérix-Where Children Come Face-to-Face with Medieval France

*60128 Plailly, France*

When you're looking for a day trip out of, but still close to Paris made just for the kids, why not try something every French child would find fascinating as well? Parc Astérix, located just 30 minutes north of Paris by car, is a theme park dedicated to the much beloved medieval characters Astérix and Obelix. These famous Gaul characters were developed in the late 1950's as a comic strip. The French quickly fell in love with quirky Astérix and Obelix as they took part in crazy adventures through medieval France.

A household name for French children, Parc Astérix is the perfect mix of theme park fun intertwined with historical relevance. Kids can take a spin on the roller coaster and follow it up with a trip through a Medieval village with Astérix. Buy your tickets ahead of time to skip the line and make sure to arrive early to make the most of your medieval day!

# Disneyland Paris-A Magical Destination

### *77777 Marne-la-Vallée, France*

If it's a guaranteed magical moment you're looking for during your stay in Paris, you'll only need to venture about 20 miles east of the city by car to find what your heart desire. Disneyland Paris, formerly known as Euro Disney opened its doors in 1992 and has been capturing the hearts of the young, old and every age in between ever since. An extension of Walt Disney's array of global theme parks, Disneyland Paris takes a European twist on the exciting Mickey-centric experience.

Broken into two sections including the infamous castle as well as a section focused on Disney movie production, the park is currently in the process of expanding even further. Park officials have recently announced they will be adding Star Wars and Frozen exhibits over the next few years! Easy to access and brimming with rides, sweets and stunning shows in between, this is another stop worth arriving to early in order to make the most of your magical day.

# Ferris Wheel Rides at the Place de la Concorde

*Place de la Concorde, 75008 Paris, France*

The Place de la Concorde is notoriously a place known for its privileged view in the city of Paris. Settled between the Champs Élysées and the Tuileries Garden, it's hard to find a place here that isn't worth a lingering gaze. So why not take that view to new heights?

The Grand Ferris Wheel offers up this exciting opportunity for the whole family. With 48 pods to choose from, you're sure to have an incredible experience and make some even better family memories while you're at it.

If you're traveling through Paris during the Christmas season, you'll want to be sure to take a spin as the wheel offers up some dazzling sights of the intricate lightwork that graces the entire length of the Champs Élysées.

# Time to Trampoline at Jardin des Tuileries

*113 Rue de Rivoli, 75001 Paris, France*

The Jardin des Tuileries is the green gateway to the Louvre for many tourists. Leading up to the grand museum, it can be hard to stop and look around as the great masters of art both past and present, summon you their way. When it comes to activities for the kids in Paris however, the Jardin des Tuileries is a prime place for fun and excitement, if you're willing to take a pause along your path.

From time to time, you'll find pop up puppet shows to captivate your child's imagination, so keep your eyes open as you wander those graveled paths. If you are exploring Paris in the summer, you may even stumble upon the opportunity for a quick pony ride in the park. However, the hidden highlight of the Tuileries is definitely the in-ground trampolines available for children to take their play to new heights. Perfect for running, jumping and flipping around when the inspiration calls, these bouncing runways are ideal for giving energy a scenic outlet in the City of Light.

# Chapter 10: Shopping Stops for the Fashion Lover

As much as it is renowned for it's history, art and overwhelmingly delicious flavor, Paris is also a first class stop for global fashionistas. Fortunately, Paris is as diverse when it comes to it's consumer products as it is with its pastries and museums.

Contrary to some belief systems, you don't actually have to be a millionaire to appreciate the Parisian shopping experience. Whether you're looking for Chanel or vintage posters, Louis Vuitton or King Louis inspired magnets, there's a little something for everyone as you shop your way through Paris.

## Les Halles

### 101 rue Berger, 75001 Paris, France

Les Halles is an infamous underground shopping mall that acts as a poster child for the very idea of Parisian structural transformation. What began as the central food distribution hub in the city hundreds of years ago has seamlessly been transformed into the center for consumerism that it is today.

Uniquely modern with its steel beam and glass architecture crafted by Victor Baltard in the 1950's, this modernized structure surrounds and covers a moderately priced shopping center for those with an eye for all that is trendy. Stopping here gives you the opportunity to find everything from kitchen ware to casual chic clothing and even a LEGO store for the little ones when entertainment is top of mind.

# Bon Marché

*24 Rue de Sèvres, 75007 Paris, France*

It's very likely you've experienced a department store or two in your day, but when it comes to department stores with history and class to boot, nobody does it quite like Bon Marché. Nestled into the left bank of the 7th arrondissement, Bon Marché stands as a symbol of luxury in the heart of Paris. Established in 1838, Bon Marché holds the title of oldest department store, but don't let that fool you in the least.

While it's roots may be historic, this department store carries brands that are anything but passé. Innovative, modern and at the cutting edge of luxury products, this is the place to find all of your name brand clothing pieces. Glamorous down to it's very intricate stone architecture, the Bon Marché is a piece of the past that refuses to be recognized as anything other than fashion forward.

# Boulevard Saint Germain-des-Prés

## Boulevard Saint Germain-des-Prés, 75007 Paris, France

When you're hunting for more of an overall shopping experience instead of a single stop shop, it's imperative that you make your way towards Boulevard Saint Germain-des-Prés. The boulevard itself is lined with a seemingly endless string of stores and shops that host everything from Armani to H&M. The fun in discovering this consumer route is that not only is there an opportunity to find that perfect something you've been searching for, but you have a chance to explore an entire neighborhood along the way!

Often referred to by Parisians as Bobo-Chic, this area is known for attracting those shoppers who appreciate the balance between luxury and trendy. This is perfect if you're someone who loves to admire high end fashion right alongside charming, ready-to-wear boutiques. With price points tailored to an essential rainbow of budgets, this is an all-for-one shopping experience that gives you a glimpse of all the best Paris has to offer.

# Avenue Georges V

## Avenue George V, 75008 Paris, France

Stretched alongside the glittering Champs Élysées and playing host to one of Paris's most luxurious and costly hotels, Avenue Georges V is an opportunity for those without budget constraints, or those who lovingly admire the luxurious style of the rich and famous.

The Four Seasons George V Hotel, often referred to just as the George V, is a top tier hotel to those for whom price is not an issue. While it is a centerpiece of the street, the avenue itself is oozing with luxury and refinery. You will be hard pressed to find any brand name item that can't compete with Armani at the very least. If it's Hermès or Chanel you desire, Avenue George V is sure to live up to any and all expectations. If you're not in the market for spending, simply take a stroll as you link up with the Champs Élysées and bask in the lap of luxury for a brief while.

# Champs Élysées

### *Avenue des Champs-Élysées, 75008 Paris, France*

Rounding the corner from Avenue Georges V, one finds themselves standing squarely on the Champs Élysées and it's here that the world of shopping opens itself up to the more moderately priced consumer in comparison. Be prepared to face the crowds head on as this is inevitably one of the most famous and frequently visited streets in Paris. With views of the Arc de Triomphe as well as the Place de la Concorde on either end, this section of the 8th arrondissement is too convenient to be ignored. Bustling, lively and large, you'll be hard pressed to find a moment when the Champs Élysées isn't buzzing with energy!

When it comes to shopping opportunities, you'll find a pleasant mix of options and price points. If you're still in the mood for luxury brands, swing by Louis Vuitton which is illuminated with neon lights along it's sleek silver facade and hard to miss. With jewelry shops sprinkled between souvenir stores you'll find browsing the goods an easy task. When you're done, simply choose a café to sit and sip something sweet or energizing while the tourists and Parisians pass you by.

# Souvenir Central: Montmartre

*Metro Anvers, 68 Bd de Rochechouart,75009 Paris, France*

The experience of Montmartre and Sacré Coeur are priceless, but if you do intend to spend, the path up the infamous hill is lined with souvenir-esque possibilities. In fact, it's difficult to find a street from the metro stop *Anvers or Abbesses* up towards the infamous basilica that doesn't offer up a plethora of souvenir stores. These locales are packed floor to ceiling and provide everything from Picasso themed book bags to miniature Eiffel towers alongside charming music boxes that play French favorites. It's the ideal route to picking out that perfect post card to send home or finding those Parisian trinkets that are easy to pack and fun to remember your trip by.

If you're looking for something to grace your walls at home with a touch of vintage France, purchase a print of one of the many French advertisements that combine the fanciful and fun side of a biscuit or beverage. The most identifiable works and advertisements of famed artist Henri de Toulouse-Lautrec fill the street corner shops in bold colored prints.

If you're looking to personalize you adventure, there are always a string of street artists at the top of the hill eager to sketch your likeness for a price. Arriving from all artistic backgrounds and skill levels, it's worth your time to watch before you volunteer to be the model of the moment.

# Clignancourt Flea Market-Les Puces

### *Avenue de la Porte de Clignancourt, 75018 Paris, France*

When the weekend rolls around and you're itching to explore the antiques aisle, there's only one place to be. The largest flea market in Paris is hosted at the Porte de Clignancourt and shouldn't be missed, if merely for the witnessing of this spectacular event. Starting at 9 am on Saturdays and 10 am on Sundays, this is not an antique shopping stop for the faint of heart.

Be prepared to encounter a bustling, lively experience with endless possibilities for finding treasures along the way. From silverware to jewelry, vintage plates to one-of-a-kind fabrics, this flea market lovingly referred to as *Les Puces,* provides an atmosphere uniquely its own. Whether you're a collector of shining house keys or prefer to ponder painting after painting, this flea market makes a name for itself based on sheer size, volume and opportunities for antique adventures!

## Les Cléfs d'Or Concierge and Shopping Service

It's possible to be given every tip and trick in the book and still find yourself drowning in the sea of shopping that is the city of Paris. Even those with a clear view of what they are after can find themselves overwhelmed by the sheer volume of possibilities from time to time. Before panic sets in, be sure to ask your hotel front desk expert about the possibility of speaking with someone associated with Les Cléfs d'Or.

The name translates literally into *The Golden Keys* and it stands to reason. The organization is comprised of a highly trained group of professional concierges. Working strategically in many hotels throughout Paris and across the globe, these individuals are educated in the art of being a local expert and guide. Working all over the world, you can rest assured that if you are speaking with a concierge who wears the Golden Keys, you are getting the very best insight into the heart and soul of the city no matter if you're looking for information on shopping, sightseeing or dining experiences crafted to dazzle the palate. Don't be shy when it comes to asking for a Clefs d'Or Concierge. It's an incredible strategy when you're looking for ways to maximize your time and experience in a city and you're tight on the schedule.

If you have a moment before you travel, you can always contact a representative directly. Working internationally to provide top class service and authentic insight, it's worth taking the time to contact them and see how you can add some flavor and fun to the travel list you've already built for your adventure abroad.

# Chapter 11: Hotels You Can't Miss

There is a modern trend across continents that allows travelers to easily rent personal apartments as they skip across countries. Similarly, if you're even more willing to put amenities to the side, you can consider couch surfing your way across the world. While these options are always available, there's just something about hotel life in Paris that should be experienced when you visit the City of Light and Love. A culture all unto its own, the very art of hospitality is renowned in Paris and the career path of professional accommodation is pursued with passion by a vast number of Parisians.

Considering the heights to which hospitality is revered as well as the pleasure of experiencing these incredible locations Paris has to offer up, it's worth the investment to spend some time admiring and making the most of these note-worthy hotels.

## George V

### *31, avenue George V, 75008 Paris, France*

Officially known as the Four Seasons George V Hotel, a stay at this Parisian landmark is a visit to the very lap of luxury. It's hard to separate this fine establishment from thoughts of celebrity and class. Directly off the Champs Élysées and Hermés and Chanel adjacent, the George V requires a large budget but asks for an even larger appreciation for the finer things in life in return.

Immense in every possible way, the George V boasts both an architecture and standard of hospitality that demands superior attention. Elegant, charming and accommodating, the staff at the George V are the crème de la crème, handpicked from an impressive pool of highly educated hospitality experts in Paris and from around the globe. Their expertise is put to work as they assist and welcome guests to a world of seductive elegance.

With endless and awe inspiring floral arrangements everywhere you look, the George V is beautiful wonder to behold. Draped in fine silks and complete with glossy marble, the hotel itself is dressed in the best. With full apartment-style suites that come complete with balconies and scenic views of the city, there isn't detail left to chance. When hunger comes calling, you have the choice between three Michelin star restaurants including Le George, L'Orangerie or Le Cinq.

The George V can cater to every desire and indulgence possible during your stay. From a full day spa to childcare services and family activities available in between any and all of your plans, there's something for everyone when you're spending time with the Four Seasons family.

# Hotel La Comtesse

## *9 Avenue de Tourville, 75007 Paris, France*

When you're looking for an authentic Parisian hotel experience that's reasonably priced but superior on the location and view front, look no further than the Hotel La Comtesse. Nestled into the heart of the 7th arrondissement, this hotel brings comfort, views and convenient location to the forefront of your Paris stay.

Fully renovated in 2016, La Comtesse is both exceptionally elegant and extremely comfortable for individual travelers and families alike. Complete with its own namesake café for the best in dining and people watching, it's truly a complete all-in-one stay.

With rooms that include gorgeous wrought-iron balconies and exceptional views of the Eiffel Tower and bustling École Militaire below, you're hard pressed to find a room that doesn't satisfy the senses on every level. Don't hesitate to ask the multilingual staff for their best advice on where to go and what to do on any given day under the sun during your stay. Passionate about their profession and the city they love, you'll find some of the best insider advice at La Comtesse time and again.

# Hotel Eiffel Rive Gauche

*6 Rue du Gros Caillou, 75007 Paris, France*

While Paris is a city that most definitely offers up hotel experiences for those who hold space and spa-centric extras at the top of the list, there is an entirely different side of Paris to be experienced as well when it comes to picking the perfect hotel for your stay. Old Paris glam is more about charm and delicate details than luxurious living. Snuggled on a hidden away corner of Rue du Gros Caillou in the 7th, no more than a two-minute walk from the Eiffel Tower stands the Hotel Eiffel Rive Gauche.

This hotel is worth discovering for the old-world Parisian atmosphere it offers up from the moment you walk through the door. Stepping off the cobblestones and into the front lobby, you'll be greeted by a warm atmosphere stemming from the decorative color scheme to multilinguistic catering the staff impressively delivers to guests. It's hard not to admire the elegance of the large mahogany desk that takes center stage of the front lobby.

Complete with welcoming yellow walls, black and white checkered floors and cushy red chairs, this hotel takes you back to a time when charm, atmosphere and creativity reigned supreme. A narrow winding staircase leads you up to rooms that open onto neighborhood views gazing over the silvery rooftops of Paris. Within the span of a heartbeat, it's possible to feel the very pulse of Paris in this place.

Make sure to note the miniature indoor courtyard complete with cobblestones as you make your way from your room to the dining area on the ground floor. A buffet style breakfast and café crème in the morning sets you well on your way to a Parisian adventure like no other.

# Hotel Ritz Paris

*15 Place Vendôme, 75001 Paris, France*

As diverse as the neighborhoods of Paris itself, the hotel life of the city buzzes with opportunity. For those seeking a trendy-chic stay in Paris, disappointment is nowhere to be found. If you're willing to set budget aside for a short while, the Hotel Ritz Paris is waiting to offer up an extravagant stay option under a well-known name in the 1st arrondissement.

Some of the most infamous ex-pats Paris has called her own spent quality time at the Ritz, both perfecting their crafts and mingling with those who were on similar paths in life. From Gertrude Stein to F. Scott Fitzgerald, staying at the Ritz is an exercise in following the footsteps of some of the greatest literary minds the world has ever known. Known to inspire with the combination of it's lively culinary and artistic endeavors as well as it's elegant décor that speaks to an enviable time passed, the Ritz sets you back to the 1920's while offering up the best of 21st century amenities.

Between haute couture exhibitions, exquisite culinary options, the opportunity to browse The Great Library or sip something sweet at the Ritz Bar, you'll easily fill your days to the very heartbeat of Paris. When you're looking for a brief pause, tea time at the Salon Proust is not to be missed.

# Shangri-La Paris

*10 Avenue d'Iéna, 75116 Paris, France*

One of the unique abilities Paris possesses is her incredible knack for reflecting the glamorous past into the ravishingly innovative future. Perhaps no hotel in Paris does this as exquisitely seamlessly as the Shangri-La Paris tucked squarely into the chic 16th arrondissement. Where France's past notoriously gives credit to Napoleon Bonaparte, this hotel has taken the idea of Napoleonic homage to a new level by being constructed in the very residence of Napoleon's grandnephew, Prince Roland Bonaparte.

While the hotel falls on the high price point end of luxurious stays, the cost comes with equally grand rewards. Crafted squarely around the concept of royalty and all that is regale, the atmosphere at Shangri-La Paris exudes elegance and all things fine from the moment you walk in to the second you check out. With interior décor made to mirror the old-world refinement of Paris, you're sure to encounter gold gilding, lush fabrics, impressive crystal chandeliers and every decorative luxury in between.

The hotel's bar is known for their signature Pink Lady drink that's equally pleasing to the eye and taste buds. While high end shopping stops on Avenue George V are just around the corner, you can just as easily spend an afternoon admiring the city from your room's roof top vantage point. Looking out over Trocadero, shimmering Seine and the Eiffel Tower, it's not hard to lose yourself in the elegance and class as well as the feeling you've been elevated to the status of pure royalty when you stay at the Shangri-La Paris.

# Chapter 12: Places Famous for Those Whose Hearts Beat for Art

## Les Deux Magots

*6 Place Saint Germain- des-Prés, 75006 Paris, France*

It's not uncommon for inspiration to hit over a drink. Where friends and frivolity collide, there is often room for a creative spirit to overtake. For this reason, amongst many more, the literary greats of the last few centuries would often convene at Les Deux Magots to contemplate their work or simply spend time together. Today, this jewel of the 6th arrondissement is a popular tourist hangout but shouldn't be missed as it's impossible to stop by and not be in awe of the fact that some of the greatest writers history has offered up spent their days and nights in this very establishment.

This church front café gives off a distinctly old Paris feel as you sip your beer, hot chocolate or rosé street side or at an interior booth. With floor to ceiling windows dressed up in heavy curtains and gold gilded lighting above your head, it's not hard to imagine Hemingway, Sartre, Stein or Wilde writing steadily away in one of the deep corners of the room.

# Hotel d'Angleterre- Room 14

## *44 Rue Jacob, 75006 Paris, France*

Earnest Hemingway's love affair with Paris started young and lasted the entirety of his lifetime. Much of his writing was inspired by the city itself, and his own life continually circled back to Paris in one way or another. While his writing has captivated audiences for decades, it can be equally intriguing to retrace his steps through the City of Light.

Once you've spent some time at Les Deux Magots and sufficiently absorbed the atmosphere that gave way to Hemingway's own inspiration, why not stop by the hotel he held in such high esteem as well? Hotel d'Angleterre in the 6th arrondissement previously held the role of British Embassy up until the late 18th century when it was transformed into the hotel it is today. It was this very establishment that Hemingway and his first wife stayed at when they came to Paris in 1921.

Room 14 was assigned to them during that trip and to this day, it's possible to reserve the room for yourself. Modern Hemingway and literary buffs alike flock to the location throughout the year, so make sure to reserve in advance if you're looking for a place that's perfectly suited for a stay in Paris and unashamedly poetic.

# Picasso's Residence-Montmartre

## *11 bis rue Ravignan, Place Émile Goudeau, 75018 Paris, France*

If it's more an experience with art that gets your pulse racing, you won't want to miss a visit to one of Picasso's most well-known Parisian residence which goes by the name of Le Bateau-Lavoir. Situated in the heart of the 18th arrondissement, this location suffered devastating destruction in the 1970's when it caught fire but has since been rebuilt and the original façade remains intact to this day.

Located just below the Place du Tertre, Le Bateau-Lavoir was an ideally placed residence in the thriving artist's district of Montmartre in the creative height of the 19th and 20th centuries. Picasso, along with a plethora of other artists, authors and theater greats spent a significant amount of time here sharing ideas and creating history through an artistic lens. Today, one must understand it's significance in order to find it as it is easily passed by in the mix of an ever-growing Montmartre district. It can be hard to fathom that behind such a simple façade, incredible works such as Picasso's *Les Demoiselles D'Avignon* was born in 1907.

# Giverny

## *Rue Claude Monet, 27620 Giverny, France*

On the quiet outskirts of Paris lies an area of France known as Giverny. It was here that famous impressionist Claude Monet settled in both home and inspirational spirit during the middle of the 1800's. Complete with lush, floral gardens and glassy ponds, it was in this very place that the artist found his muse that led to the birth of works depicting the infamous footbridge and water lilies series. With a passion for horticulture and a keen sense of how color and light could dance together, this was the ideal location for Monet to delve into the finer details of what we know today as Impressionism.

Easy to complete as a half-day excursion outside of the city, a trip to Giverny is an experience in serene beauty and incredibly scenic views. As you wander through the gardens and Monet's home, it's nearly impossible to miss the sense of artistic wonder that weaves its way through each and every moment you stumble upon. Vibrant colors combined in natural floral arrangements alongside still water gives way to a glittering scene of natural awe. A trip to Giverny gives visitors a glimpse into the man that was Monet.

# Chapter 13: Seine Side Excursions

Paris has many icons, but one so central as to be a primary navigational point in the city is the Seine. Winding gently through Paris and dividing her banks into equal parts, the Seine is mysterious in the secrets it holds and a guiding force on a Parisian map. It has inspired songwriters and novelists through the centuries. Even today, there's something captivating in the power it holds as a symbol of the city itself.

While it holds the power to inspire stories, the Seine's natural path has created some of the most beloved walking routes Paris offers. Simply following the river's path will bring you to an endless string of stunning views, historical locations and adventurous activities. Here are just a few of the most note-worthy seine side paths and excursions.

## Walking Route from Towers to Spires

Finding yourself in Paris is an experience in giving up some of those transportation trends we have seemingly engrained into our very DNA. Normal life generally calls for the use of a car, but in Paris, it's entirely possible to leave your world of wheels behind and stick firmly to your own two feet in order to experience the city in the most beautiful way possible.

Paris is a city of walkers, loved by land dwellers and inevitably begging you to wander it's many streets. While it's considered a large city, you'll hear Parisians time and again refer to it as a "small" big city. This is mostly due to its comprehensive layout. Paris holds millions of residents but maintains the feel of a familiar village as you move seamlessly from neighborhood to neighborhood. Many of the major landmarks share space within a mile or two of one another and for this reason, your walks are never without awe-inspiring moments.

If you're looking to stroll and find your very French fascination simultaneously, it's an easy choice. Starting at the base of the Eiffel Tower you'll simply follow the river in the direction of crossing Avenue de la Bourdonnais. It may sound too simple to be true, but some things in Paris are as direct as they seem-- this serene and scenic route being one of them. As you wander along the left bank of the Seine you'll be privy to some of Paris' most iconic sights, all while maintaining a leisurely pace. Feel free to let inspiration fly as you walk past Les Invalides, the Musée d'Orsay and experience breathtaking views of the massive Louvre where she sits majestically on the other side of the river.

Less than 2 miles from your starting point, you'll encounter the Place St. Michel with its impressive fountain and lively café plaza. It's here that the Pont St. Michel offers you a crossing point with direct access to Notre Dame. With its white stone façade reaching into the Parisian sky, it's hard not to feel you've gotten the inside scoop on what it means to capture the City of Light when you make time to take this walking route along the Seine.

# Trocadéro Aquarium

## *5 Avenue Albert de Mun, 75016 Paris, France*

Travelers flock to Paris with visions of towers and arches swimming in their heads, but what's most intriguing about the city is the unexpected pleasures that could be swimming by in real time as well. While it might not be your first thought, it should definitely be a stop along the way. The aquarium of Paris, officially called Aquarium de Paris-Cinéaqua is hidden away between the 7th and 16th arrondissements just beside the Trocadéro which is normally teeming with tourists.

One of the best kept secrets of this infamous area, the aquarium is ideal for a fun afternoon with the family or even a quiet romantic rendezvous with the one you love. Colorful, attractively spacious and noticeably peaceful, you might forget you're in one of the most popular tourist destination on the planet for a while. Complete with a shark tunnel, hundreds of glittering tanks and a cinema, the aquarium is an underwater oasis just a step away from the most iconic symbol France offers up to the world.

# Bateaux Mouches River Cruise

## *Port de la Conférence, 75008 Paris, France*

Parisians know at heart that the best view of Paris by far comes from the river Seine itself. Capitalizing on this opportunity, Bateaux Mouches is your one stop shop for Seine River Cruises that gives you not only the best views of the city but adds the most flavor and entertainment to your experience as well.

With lunch, brunch and romantic dinner options to choose from, Bateaux Mouches gives you the opportunity to dine when and how you want to, all while experiencing some of the most breathtaking views Paris has to offer. You'll pass by the Louvre, Musée d'Orsay, Notre-Dame and come back to a glittering Eiffel Tower if you've chosen the evening route.

For an even more exciting experience, ask about the dinner and show options that are available. While onboard musicians keep your ears tingling during each dinner experience, Bateaux Mouches also delivers up the chance to exit at Paris's infamous Crazy Horse or Moulin Rouge for some risqué entertainment once dinner is done. Gourmet meals, constant attention to detail and a view that frames the city of Paris in her best light makes this an unforgettable experience.

# Rent it to Believe it-House Boats on the Seine

While many travelers to Paris will opt for the home share or hotel route to accommodate their stay, there is another, more overlooked option sitting right on the Seine itself. For those who seek an experience with a unique domestic twist, it's imperative to note that those charming house boats you encounter as you walk along the Seine are not all under personal contract. In fact, many are open for rental and can create a fun and whimsical escape during your time in Paris.

While it's possible to look for individual owners posting rental possibilities before you take off on your journey, there are several agencies in Paris that provide contracts for short term houseboat rentals. Some of these include parisattitude.com or bookahouseboat.com.

Whichever route you take to setting up your stay, you're sure to have an experience that's out of the ordinary and splashes into the heart of your Parisian adventure. With incredible views and access to all major monuments, these houseboats are an incredible way to not only see but stay in the city.

# Bridges to Leave Footprints Over and Under

Walking through Paris, more specifically as you follow the Seine, inevitably brings you to some of the most beautiful and historically significant monuments imaginable. Seeped in centuries of history and architectural advancement, Paris is a testament to ages gone by while simultaneously wrapping herself in innovative approaches to life.

This same level of past and present can be seen in the bridges that connect the city across the Seine. These are the points in Paris that connect pathways, sides of life and bridge people together. They are worth admiring and leaving your own footprints on as you get to know a city so many have fallen in love with before you ever arrived.

**Pont Alexandre III:** When you're looking for aesthetic wonder, look no further than Pont Alexandre III. Construction began in 1896 and since that time, it's captivated admirers with it's elegant gold gilding and extravagant stonework. Its glittering arch connects Les Invalides with the Champs Élysées making it a well-traveled and fashionable bridge between Parisian landmarks. Complete with golden topped pillars and bronze triple tiered light posts, you'll feel compelled to high class living, even if just for the crossing.

**Pont Neuf:** Don't let the name, which translates to *New Bridge* fool you as this is the oldest bridge in Paris. Construction on this historic Parisian crossing first began in 1578 and has remained a dominating presence ever since. Medieval architectural influence leaves us today with a bridge that is robust and authentic in it's longevity.

Massive arches allow river boats to pass underneath with ease while rounded braces give the impressive you're walking across the top of old castle walls. Connecting the left and right banks of the Île de la Cité, Pont Neuf sits at was once upon a time, the very birthplace of Paris.

**Pont des Arts:** Sometimes the beauty in stepping into a place is simply to be standing on ground that has endured seemingly impossible moments in history. The Pont des Arts pedestrian bridge is today an artistic crafting of wood and steel that was redone in the mid 1980's after weakening under the stress of impacts endured throughout World Wars I and II. Once refurbished, this bridge has remained a highlight of Parisian culture, connecting river banks at the Louvre and Institute de France.

Many travelers recognize the bridge as one that use to host an endless number of *love locks*. Tourists and Parisians alike would profess their feelings and write their names on a lock before attaching it to the bridge and throwing the key away in the river in the hopes of securing a guarantee of an enduring love. While this gesture was romantic, it was also stressful to the architectural integrity of the bridge itself as well as being environmentally damaging to the Seine. The city of Paris banned love locks when it finally looked as though the bridge itself would suffer and potentially collapse. Still, the sentiment remains and it's worth taking a trip over the bridge in the name of love.

# Chapter 14: Theaters That Bring the Dramatic City to Life and Stage

Travelers fall in love with Paris for reasons as diverse as the story of the city itself. From the flavor of foods that bring your taste buds to life, to the rich history that seems to be waiting around every stone corner, there's hardly a piece of Paris that doesn't match up with someone's interest or passion. While some will search for the heart of fashion, others crave the endless art so readily available to be consumed by the senses. Yet hovering above it all and connecting these desires at their core is Paris's innate gift to entertain.

Whether it's by way of the mind, the eye or the tongue, Paris has a way of taking reality and crafting it into something exquisite that captivates long after you've left the city limits. As you get to know Paris, it's worth acknowledging this powerful gift and giving it some time and attention. Entertainment that was born here centuries ago still thrives alongside modern mechanism of diversion, and the experience is just as invigorating today as it was in the once upon a time.

## Palais Garnier

*8 Rue Scribe, 75009 Paris, France*

Completed in 1875, this substantial musical icon of Paris is hard to miss as you wander through the 9th arrondissement. Designed by Charles Garnier, the

Palais Garnier was and still is, the premier Opera and ballet house of Paris. Even if you're not overwhelmed by music or dance, this is a feat of architecture worth admiring. From golden gilded sculpture to soaring, glittering ceilings complete with belle époque style paintings, the vast and bold presence of this opera house is stunning.

Today, the establishment primarily hosts ballet within it's glamorous walls and is available to be toured. As you enter the building, you'll be washed in wonder at the sheer luxury of the grand staircase that meets you and winds up several floors. Built to sustain and maintain the ultimate acoustic and visual opportunities, the Palais Garnier stands to impress.

# Grand Rex

### *1 Boulevard Poissonnière, 75002 Paris, France*

Cinema and theater have long been important past times in Paris. French culture has delivered up timeless cinematic treasures and some of the most important names in the business as well. The Grand Rex in the 2nd arrondissement brings the best of both of these worlds together.

Originally designed to be the most beautiful and impressive theater in Paris, today the Rex is the unique combination of charming stage set and over-the-top theater production. You can book tickets for the latest movie releases or purchase tickets for a live show. Most impressively, this location gives off an atmosphere of both old Hollywood and Disney as it dazzles you with starry ceilings and intricate architectural work to frame each screen and stage. With glittering lights and a fantastic sense of stepping into the heart of entertainment, the Grand Rex is a must-see for movie and theater lovers everywhere.

# Cirque d'Hiver

*110 Rue Amelot, 75011 Paris, France*

There's nothing like a visit to the circus to bring your childhood roaring back to life right before your eyes. Parisians long ago acknowledged the power of this magical experience which involves bringing together the exotic, daring and entertaining. The result was the Cirque d'Hiver located in the 11th arrondissement.

Completed in 1952, it was originally named Cirque Napoleon but transitioned to it's current name as of 1970. What makes the entire concept so fascinating is that it takes everything that's temporary about the circus concept and makes it a permanent establishment of fun in the heart of this neighborhood. Built with 20 stone sides meant to reflect the feeling of entering a massive circus tent, the structure even possesses a tent-like roof. Walking in, it's impossible to distinguish the mobile past from this present one rooted in stone reality. Colorful, bright and brimming with entertainment, the Cirque d'Hiver plays host to not only the circus, but many interesting exhibitions and concerts throughout the year as well.

# Crazy Horse

*12 Avenue George V, 75008 Paris, France*

Paris is associated with everything from fine dining to art and the incredible history that flows between it all. That being said, it's hard to separate Paris from a bit of it's risqué culture as well and that's where Crazy Horse comes into the picture. Opening it's red, sparkling doors to the public in 1951, Crazy Horse is one of Paris's top cabaret establishments.

Running several shows daily, Crazy Horse delivers the best the world of Burlesque has to offer with an assortment of 90-minute shows featuring a range of performances and of course, nudity. While dinner isn't offered here, you can expect to be graced with extraordinary musical interludes between sets and endless entertainment alongside a drink or two.

Where as once upon a time the shows tended to offer up a cast that ultimately fit into the same visual categories, these days with new management at the helm, the Crazy Horse has earned a fun reputation for inviting big name guests to come and star in their performances. Some of these individuals in the past have included Pamela Anderson, Dita Von Tesse, Carmen Electra and many more! If you're in the mood for a daring date night out, the Crazy Horse is a good add to your agenda and you never know who might be making their way on stage.

# Moulin Rouge

## *82 Boulevard de Clichy, 75018 Paris, France*

It's been honored in song and in cinema and with it's iconic red windmill boldly turning, has become a household name across the globe and remains a pride point of Paris today. The Moulin Rouge has an almost mysterious allure that draws visitors to it's doors by the hundreds.

Recognized as the birthplace of the can-can, the Moulin Rouge continues to run as a cabaret to this very day. Appropriately positioned in the seedy Pigalle district, the Moulin Rouge fascinates visitors with its floor to ceiling aura of old-Paris décor alongside that sense of scandal that accompanies a visit to the infamous burlesque show. There's something exquisite about a visit to the location that inspired Henri de Toulouse-Lautrec's notorious advertisements.

Beyond the aesthetics, there is a longevity and history to the Moulin Rouge that's impressive. Even as Paris was under siege during WWII, the performers and artistic minds behind the cabaret maintained a sense of responsibility. The phrase *"the show must go on"* was nothing less than a lifeblood mantra as the Moulin Rouge managed to keep its doors open throughout the war. Today, it's a symbol of fun and lasting vitality for tourists and Parisians alike who enter through its doors under the glow of enduring red, neon lights.

# Champs Élysées Theaters

### *144-146 Av. des Champs-Élysées, 75008 Paris, France*

Just a few steps from the bustling Place Charles de Gaulle Étoile on the lively Champs Élysées, you'll find an opportunity to step out of the craziness of this Parisian hot spot and into another world altogether. Movie lovers will be pleased to find that if it's an afternoon of escaping into the world of cinematic wonder you crave, the UGC George V on the Champs Élysées has just what you are looking for.

With the ability to screen 16 films at once, there's sure to be something on that strikes your film fancy. Don't let language barriers put you off as films are shown in both their original language with subtitles or with the option to view the newest films on the market dubbed in French when you're willing to put your linguistic skills to the test. Providing films in 3-D and every viewing option in between, a few hours of losing yourself in the world of cinematic sensation could be just what is called for.

# Chapter 15: City Views Worth Finding

Fans of Paris flock to her city limits with a desire for experience. Travelers and Parisians alike long to carve out their own space in the city through both the tactile and textural senses. There's seemingly an underlying ache within the population to know this place through it's many stories, it's ancient architecture and its delightful flavors that arrive on the tongue in a rainbow of colors. These very tangible moments do make Paris the city it is, but sometimes, it's not about what we can grasp or taste that makes Paris the most memorable. Sometimes, it's all about an incredible view.

Paris is a large city like so many others, but the unique layout combined with the physical ground on which the city is built provide for something spectacular. These alongside the historical landmarks that fit into the scenery like puzzle pieces makes for some truly awe-inspiring moments to simply...gaze. Paris is a city that allows for visitors to be a part of the frantic dash from place to place if they please, but equally allows for time to just see and be in the moment. There are a few places that are significantly worth making time to visit during your stay in the City of Light-- if for nothing more than just taking a moment and admiring the stunning view available to you.

# Montmartre- It's Time to Make the Climb

*35 Rue du Chevalier de la Barre, 75018 Paris, France*

It is best known for being the heart of artistic history. A past and present hub for those who crave to create, Montmartre cultivates all that is colorful and creative on a hill all its own. Difficult to miss, Montmartre also plays host to the infamous Sacré-Coeur Basilica which gleams stark and white in contrast to the soft, green hill that leads up to its towering presence. All around, street artists mingle, and quaint cafés dot the slanted side streets that maintain their cobblestone charm to this very day. With so much activity and life happening on this hillside oasis, it may be difficult to imagine finding a place to just stop and reflect, but it's worth your time to make way for a quiet moment.

Part of Montmartre's charm lies in it's heightened location. The steps that lead up to Sacré-Coeur are generally packed with the chatter of tourists and musicians but find a spot for yourself on the cool, stone slabs and it's easy to see why. The view from the top of the steps is unmatched. Gazing out onto Paris from above, you'll be thrilled to find that your view holds all the best Paris has to offer in a single frame. From the Eiffel Tower to Montparnasse, the Panthéon to Invalides, there's little that can't be spotted from this vantage point. Combine that with the scent of crêpes and coffee wafting through the air and you'll have found that you're suddenly a part of that simple Parisian moment, sprinkled with a little magic, that you've been looking for all along.

# Trocadéro- A World Fair View of Past and Present

*Place du Trocadéro, 75016 Paris, France*

Parisian landmarks are fascinating in and of themselves. With stories reaching back centuries and famous names linked to nearly every monument and boulevard, you're hard pressed to find a tourist attraction that doesn't captivate on some historical level. The most recognizable of these landmarks today is inevitably the Eiffel Tower. During any given summer afternoon, you're bound to find yourself pressed shoulder to shoulder with tourists trying to get that perfect shot of this rising landmark from all possible angles. When faced with the daunting task of carving out a place for yourself amongst the masses, try taking a trip across the Seine to Trocadéro.

While equally busy in the daytime, as evening sets in, this right bank landmark tends to thin out and becomes the most ideal vantage spot to take a breath as well as the perfect frame for capturing the Eiffel Tower's best side. Designed for the World's Fair of 1878, the Trocadéro visitors enjoy today is only a portion of its original architectural splendor. Designed as a large palace with two impressive wings on either side, today it is only the wings that remain. Fortunately, their structures hug the remaining plaza on either side and create a staggering lens through which you can observe the Eiffel Tower as well as the Chaillot gardens that stretch from Trocadéro to the river below.

As the sky turns violet behind Eiffel's masterpiece on a warm summer evening, it's hard not to be intrigued by the same view visitors to the World's Fair would have been captured by as well all those years ago. Ultimately, there's something special about observing a modern-day view that equally captivated those who inhabited the past.

# Tour Montparnasse-A Bird's Eye View on Paris

*33 Avenue du Maine, 75015 Paris, France*

While throngs of visitors scale and elevate themselves up the Eiffel Tower daily, a lesser known landmark lies just across the way. The Montparnasse tower is the second tallest building in the city of Paris and in claiming that right coveted spot, also claims to have the absolute best views of the city itself. While the view from the top of the Eiffel Tower is a bragging right everyone deserves, the view from the observation deck of the Montparnasse tower is hard to pass up. At 59 floors above the ground, it's one of the best places to not only get a bird's eye view on the entire city but capture a moment where the Eiffel Tower is on full display from above as well!

Complete with an elevator that smoothly slides visitors up to the top floor in no less than 38 seconds, it's an easy trip from ground to sky with plenty of extras to greet you once you arrive. Shining telescopes and interactive, digital neighborhood maps are waiting for visitors hoping to get a closer look at life near and far from the top of the tower. The history of Paris is written on the very walls of this space with several exhibits dedicated to fashion icons and architects that have graced Paris with their designs over generations. Stop for a coffee at the little interior café before continuing around the perimeter to experience Paris from previously unknown heights and views. Your vantage points are as endless as the seas of glass windows that creates the physical top boarder of this massive tower.

# Place de la Concorde and her Several Spectacular Views

*Place de la Concorde, 75008 Paris, France*

The Place de la Concorde is known for its towering and ancient obelisk as well as it's iconic Ferris Wheel and glittering gold and green fountains. An entry way to Rue du Rivoli and all the consumer options the street possesses, there is much to be found and even more to do in this space. One activity not to be missed as you make your way through this section of the 8th arrondissement is the simple art of observation. One of the most interesting aspects of the Place de la Concorde is its seemingly endless access to incredible views from each and every direction you can possibly turn.

The Place de la Concorde is perfectly situated to offer up views on a multitude of gorgeous sites. It's a comprehensive moment that can transform many important points of interest into one spectacular experience. Turn one way and you're face-to-face with the entrance to the Tuileries Garden, full of lush flower plots, gentle ponds and a graveled pathway directly to the Louvre. Turn to your left from there and you'll be stunned by the massive feat of architecture that is the Madeline church just down the street, easily distinguished by strong, imposing Romanesque columns and intricate stonework. Another quarter turn and you'll find you're within reach of the Champs Élysées and the Grand Palais, easily identified by the single French flag waving in the breeze above the glass dome. Another quick spin and you're eye-to-eye with the Eiffel Tower as well as the lavish left bank that frames the world leading up to the iconic landmark.

At Place de la Concorde, it can be easy to get pulled into the bustle of movement and activity that constantly graces this open space. However, rarely will you find a plaza that offers up so many opportunities for regarding life and history around you while being mesmerized by every point of view. Take a moment to stop and simply wonder at the magnitude of the frame on the city you possess when you pass this place. Once you realize you've got a vantage point on Paris that you can hardly find elsewhere, you'll be glad you did.

# La Defense and the Grand Modern Arch

*1 Parvis de la Défense, 92800 Puteaux, France*

Napoleon's mark, across several generations, is left all over the city of Paris. From bridges to buildings, it's difficult to find a spot left untouched by the boldness of Monsieur Bonaparte of any generation. One of the most recognizable works he left in his wake was the easily identifiable Arc de Triomphe. The centerpiece of the frantic Place Charles de Gaulle Etoile roundabout, this massive and impressively detailed stone arch was crafted and dedicated to the military victories Napoleon called his own.

As popular as the Eiffel Tower in many ways for tourists looking to take in the major monuments of Paris, the Arc de Triomphe has made a name entirely for itself. However, there is another arch in Paris that should be noted alongside the Arc de Triomphe. In fact, it may be La Grande Arch of La Défense that provides an even better view of the Arc de Triomphe than one could obtain standing near the landmark itself.

At the very end of metro line 1 lies the district known as La Défense. What was similarly named in honor of military achievements has today grown and transformed into the modern and innovative hub of finance and business that Paris recognizes as a great center of progress. To accompany these feats of modernity, the Grande Arch was constructed as the district's focal point in 1985. Angular, striking and sleek, this arch is the innovative counterpart to the

Arc de Triomphe that speaks to similar glories in the modern age. Visitors can choose to take an elevator up to the top for stunning interior birds eye views on the city. Alternatively, the exterior view from the ground is just as impressive. Lined up perfectly with the Arc de Triomphe, a trip to the Grande Arch of La Défense is an experience in mirror imaging as you stand between the past and present arches that Paris calls her own.

# Paris by Bike-The Value and View of Vélib

Sometimes finding the best view in Paris is a trek to one location, but what if the entire city was available to you by bike? Started in 2007, Vélib is a modern staple of Parisian transportation for those who love to cycle and is possibly the most diverse way to see the city at your own rolling pace. Ideal for those who prefer two wheels to two feet as a mode of transportation Vélib is also an incredible solution to easing the congestion and pollution of Parisian traffic. Vélib boasts of over 1,000 docking stations in the city as well as over 18,000 bicycles available for pedestrian rental.

The process is as simple as a swipe of your credit card. With payment mechanisms built into the newest electric versions of the bikes, and payment stands easily accessible as well, all it takes is a quick swipe to be off and cycling around the city. If you're up for an adventure, simply peddle the day away and return your bike at the nearest station to wherever it is you end up at the end of your hour or even your day. If you're looking for a more set itinerary, each Vélib station comes complete with a city map which lays out several potential cycling routes you could attempt.

With paths that takes you around the city's sprawling perimeter to others that stick to the heart of Paris and allow for you to cross paths with all the major monuments, your Parisian biking experience can be customized to your style, speed and taste. With close to 300 miles of bike path available to cyclists, easily aligned with some of the primary large transportation routes, there's hardly a piece of Paris that is out of reach by bike.

Similarly, the route resources offered up at Vélib stations can be equally useful for those who are more interested in seeing Paris on speedy foot than on two wheels. Runners will find that the bike paths pointed out on Vélib maps can also make for incredible treks across the city. With scenic views and endless opportunities for jogging off onto side streets to see what's happening, a run through Paris is bound to be an exciting and similarly beautiful experience.

# Chapter 16: Cemeteries for Seeking the Sacred and Serene

Visiting a large city can be physically taxing. In the pursuit of those experiences you absolutely don't want to miss in a limited amount of time, it's possible to find yourself running full speed day to day and missing some important details in the rush and fatigue. While it may not jump to mind first, a visit to some of Paris's most notable and fantastic cemeteries can be a great way to not only get to know the history of the city but slow down the pace of your trip for just a moment as well. Traveling through these sacred and serene spaces can be an incredible way to commune with the city and slow down your experience for long enough to truly absorb your time in the City of Light.

## Cimetière Montparnasse

*3 Boulevard Edgar Quinet, 75014 Paris, France*

Visible from the top of Montparnasse tower as a seemingly endless sea of small stone specks, this cemetery is Paris's second largest and potentially, most accessible by metro as it lies directly in the heart of the 14t arrondissement. Broken into easily maneuvered divisions by tree lined pathways, Cimetière Montparnasse is a respectful, stunning and peaceful oasis in the middle of Paris.

As with so many of the large cemeteries in Paris, this one was opened in the 19th century as a remedy for the overcrowded cemeteries elsewhere around the city. Today, it features a gorgeous display of both stonework and landscaping. With luscious greenery shading immaculate and intricate headstones and mausoleum entrances, it's an impressive display of memory. While you're here, make sure to locate a few notable residents including singer Serge Gainsbourg, Jean-Paul Sartre and Charles Baudelaire.

# Cimetière Montmartre

*20 Avenue Rachel, 75018 Paris, France*

Montmartre is recognized as the heart of artistic flavor and inspiration, so it's no surprise that a trip to the neighborhood's most famous cemetery would be an exercise in encountering the resting place of some of the art world's most recognizable names as well. Impressive in both size and aesthetic, Cimetière Montmartre is a sprawling green space tucked into a vibrant neighborhood in the 18th arrondissement. It is a wonderous journey of paved pathways following winding wrought iron handrails that take you on a trip through detailed stonework and breathtaking natural beauty. Tree canopies shade the graves of Emile Zola, Alexandre Dumas and Dalida just to name a few.

The Pont de Caulaincourt, otherwise known as Caulaincourt bridge, spans the entirety of this cemetery which was originally opened in 1825 and allows visitors to view the impressive maze of headstones and mausoleums from above. A visit to the interior of the cemetery gives you an up close and personal meeting with the many free roaming cats that call this space their own. The unofficial guardians of this sleepy place, you'll be pleased to find these felines frolicking about without care as you wander the many quiet alleyways Cimetière Montmartre provides.

# Père Lachaise

*16 Rue du Repos, 75020 Paris, France*

The largest of all Paris's final resting places, Père Lachaise is a unique place to visit in the center of the 20th arrondissement. Père Lachaise was established in 1804 and has grown to possess more than 70,000 plots to date. It is a highly frequented location, but do to it's sheer size, manages to remain a peaceful stop that feels hidden away from the hustle and bustle of the city. There's something about the mystique of the famous names that call Père Lachaise a final resting place alongside the stunning natural beauty the cemetery offers up that makes it an intriguing stop.

As you wander along the meticulously maintained cobblestone alleyways, the aesthetic contrast is inspiring. You'll notice a mix of massive mausoleums reaching towards the sky and tucked shoulder-to-shoulder with green, faded iron angels. As you wander through an urban sea of intricate stonework, you can't help but feel you are a witness to  the present embodiment of centuries past.

Those buried here have inspired thousands upon thousands to come pay their respects since it's 19th century inauguration. Notable names of those interred here include Oscar Wilde, Jim Morrison and Edith Piaf. Lovers of art, history, music and literature flock to the gates of Père Lachaise for the opportunity to stroll by those who made such monumental marks on their respective fields during their lifetimes.

Be sure to set aside a few quiet hours to meander through the depths of history. It's a unique opportunity to be up close with famous names of the past while being equally mesmerized by the beauty that encompasses this impressive and meaningful cemetery known as Père Lachaise.

# The Catacombs of Paris

*1 Avenue du Colonel Henri Rol-Tanguy, 75014 Paris, France*

There is so much that enchants across avenues and boulevards in Paris. More that captivates the imagination than can possibly be told as you make your way through major monuments, crisp gardens and wind your way through incredible history. However, it may be lesser known to visitors that there is an entire story to be told underneath the very ground of Paris as well.

The catacombs have long served Paris as a final resting place for residents as well as an efficient answer to overcrowded above ground cemeteries and a mystical world all of their own since their opening in 1786. An intricate tunnel system crafted out of former quarries, the catacombs are structured to contain over 6 million remains to date. Ancient bones cover the walls, cutouts and stone pathways from top to bottom and within tastefully positioned designs.

Today, a small portion of the catacombs is accessible for guided visits. It's important to note that at 130 steps underground in confined tunnels, a visit like this is perfect for those with an adventurous, inquisitive spirit and little aversion to small spaces. Do note that those under 14 are required to visit with an adult.

# Cimetière Passy

*2 Rue du Commandant Schloesing, 75016 Paris, France*

The 16th arrondissement of today has a reputation for wealth, culture and class. It's not surprising then that Cimetière Passy, which is tucked away in this very green and notably gorgeous neighborhood, would have a similar reputation it maintains. With views of the Eiffel Tower stretching over its perimeter, Cimetière Passy was quickly identified during the early 19th century as an ideal location for the aristocracy of Paris to claim as a final resting place.

Visible from the back side of Trocadéro, Cimetière Passy is a refreshing and manageable walk through as you admire the colorful and pristine arrangement of glistening headstones patchworked with shining statues and impressive mausoleums. Immaculately cared for and adorned with luscious trees and greenery, Cimetière Passy is an oasis of peace and tranquility nestled within the heart of Parisian wealth.

# Chapter 17: Castles, Kings and the Churches Between

## Basilique de St. Denis

*1 Rue de la Légion d'Honneur, 93200 Saint-Denis, France*

Just a short stop north from bustling city center Paris into the suburb of St. Denis stands a majestic testament to royal lineage and gothic architecture. The St. Denis Basilica is a stunning work of religion and art that over time, has come to host the remains of over 75 kings and queens of France as a final resting place.

While still referred to as a basilica in passing, the structure was technically promoted to the title of cathedral in 1966. Reaching with unmatched majesty towards the sky, the cathedral is awe inspiring both inside and out. Your visit here comes complete with a spectacular combination of vaulted ceilings, stained glass windows and a sprawling collection of funerary sculptures and statues to commemorate those who lie below. With opportunities to visit both the crypt as well as the main sanctuary, there's an atmosphere of intrigue and pastime that permeates an experience at the St. Denis Basilica.

# Château de Vincennes

*Avenue de Paris, 94300 Vincennes, France*

It's not often that one travels to Paris in search of a castle, but this fascinating city is full of surprises and a when a castle is called for, Paris doesn't disappoint. At the end of metro line 1, completely opposite La Défense, lies metro stop Chateau de Vincennes and it delivers up exactly what the name promises. The castle of Vincennes is today the headquarters of the French armed forces historical services, but a stop here takes visitors back in time to when this very castle hosted the French monarchy. The following years saw the castle transformed into a prison and eventually, the headquarters it is now, but ultimately, the structure has roots dating back to the 12th century as a princely hunting lodge.

With a history that boosts continuously of being a sanctuary of military might and point of protection for the city of Paris, Chateau de Vincennes is a unique look into the past while visiting present day Paris. A ticket will get you a guided visit to both the spired gothic chapel that once housed religious relics as well as the dungeons. If you don't feel like doing a guided tour, an independent stroll of the castle grounds is just as interesting and equally engaging. After passing over the deep grass covered moat and crossing the draw bridge at the entrance, you'll be thrilled to find your self in the middle of a sprawling green and cobblestone courtyard. This space allows for views of the chapel, soaring walls and white stoned keep towers.

# Château de Fontainebleau

*77300 Fontainebleau, France*

When it comes to history, longevity carries weight and no other castle in France can quite keep up on the long-distance front when compared to Château de Fontainebleau. Over the course of eight centuries, this castle was maintained as a primary residence for some of the most notable monarchs in France including Bourbons and Bonaparte amongst many more.

Massive in size and regal in demeanor, the castle of Fontainebleau is nothing less than awe inspiring and a testament to the many families, generations, styles and events the location has witnessed over time. The transformation of architectural style between the 12th and 19th century is built into the very foundation of this place and can be seen transitioning as you move from room to room. From elegant turn of the century décor aligned with gilded ceilings to gothic movement stonework, it's easy to imagine the many faces and creative inspirations that roamed the very halls beneath your feet and rooms around you.

Because of the sheer diversity of style, art and architecture available as well as the impressive history of the castle itself, today, four major museums are hosted at this residence. These include the Napoleon museum, a paintings gallery, a furniture gallery as well as the Empress Chinese museum.

One of the most recognizable and impressive feats of architecture the castle possesses is the iconic horseshoe staircase that winds down the back of the castle to the courtyard. Both intricate and elegant in design, it is a definite highlight of a trip to Château de Fontainebleau.

# Château de Versailles

*Place d'Armes, 78000 Versailles, France*

What was once recognized as the most luxurious of residences is today identified as one of the most luxurious tourist destinations in France. Just outside of Paris stands an icon recognizable as the very image of wealth, extravagance and all that glitters in gold.

The Château de Versailles is a sprawling testament to the life of royals who could have written the very book on what extravagant living is meant to look like. Today, the château can be reached in a mere 40 minutes by train and continues to enamor those who visit both it's primary residence and luxurious gardens. Wrapping around approximately 209,000 square feet, it's a true force to be reckoned with.

What began as an establishment of high court and government within the gold gilded walls in 1682 by Louis XIV only continued to grow in grandeur all the way through the French revolution. During this time, the Château de Versailles gathered and wrapped itself in gold, jewels, glitz and glamour. From the enchanting hall of mirrors to soaring bedposts, glittering chandeliers and every grandiose item of décor in between, there is not an inch of space left untouched by high class aesthetic influence. This over-the-top approach is perfectly preserved today and creates for an atmosphere of exaggerated sophistication that has a tendency to become completely mesmerizing. With 2,300 rooms to spare, a visit to the Château de Versailles requires a bit of time and a willingness to be wowed.

Once you've made your way through the château, it's time to continue on through the impressive gardens. Complete with exotic greenery imported from around the globe in the fashion of many French kings, as well as bushes cut to perfection and finished off with intricate design standards by a highly trained landscape team, the gardens seemingly take on a life of their very own. Meticulous, majestic and full of texture and endless vibrant color-you'll feel you've stepped into a wonderland of natural beauty just outside the château walls.

# Basilique du Sacré-Coeur de Montmartre

*35 Rue du Chevalier de la Barre, 75018 Paris, France*

Religion often calls for followers to take a moment to look up and recognize the power above them, and no other church in Paris demands this as physically as Sacré-Coeur which dominates the landscape of the 18th arrondissement. Placed boldly at the top of the butte Montmartre, this simultaneous basilica and catholic church are a center piece of the highest land point of the city of Paris.

Completed in 1914, Sacré-Coeur is a bit of a mix when it comes to meaning. Originally crafted as a tribute to those who lost their lives in the Franco-Prussian war, it is dually sanctified as a church dedicated to Jesus Christ. This is unique in that the majority of catholic churches created around the same time were strictly dedicated to the Virgin Mary.

Sacré-Coeur continues its tradition of standing out in a unique fashion with the very stone it stands on. Sparkling in stunning white on the top of this green hill in the most artistic district in Paris, the church was crafted with a particular travertine stone that becomes white on contact with water. Ultimately, this allows Sacré-Coeur to shine even in the gloomiest of weather. The interior and exterior architecture tend to feel softer than their gothic counterparts, however, the impressive aesthetic points are comparable. From vibrant stained-glass windows to detailed stone statues depicting important biblical moments as well as gently vaulted ceilings, the church itself is an artistic masterpiece.

Mass is held regularly during visiting hours and tourists are welcome to quietly witness the proceedings from pews lined up throughout the sanctuary. A full-scale model of the church located just behind the alter gives visitors a bird's eye view of exactly how impressive this meaningful feat of architecture is from every possible angle.

# Chapter 18: The Must-See Major Monuments Before You Leave

For all of the excitement discovering off the beaten path locations provides for visitors in Paris, there is something fundamental when traveling about coming face to face with some of the big names as well. Paris is endlessly intriguing because she is full of tantalizing secrets. It's never certain just how many new restaurants you'll stumble across as you meander the many avenues. It's never guaranteed that the little bakery you stopped at last year will be there this year, still glittering with colorful pastries in the window.

The possibilities only grow as to whom you'll potentially meet as you wander the many enchanting boulevards that stretch from one side of the city to the other. Who knows what memories are made as you cross a bridge and back, giving the Seine a piece of your heart along the way. Not much can be known in advance when you're on an adventure in the City of Light. In fact, the only thing that one can be entirely certain of are a few very important staple icons that give the city a foundational flavor all its own.

Just because they draw large numbers of tourists in doesn't mean they should be counted out when you're creating your must-see list. On the contrary, it's equally important to experience those places in any given city or country that have worked to craft a name and reputation for themselves. There's a reason the mystique has grown around these landmarks and every traveler deserves to find themselves in the glow of these prestigious and popular sites at least once in their lifetime.

Considering the essential experience, feel free to let go of expectations for a moment and be willing to leave your own mark on these Parisian sites that fill out guide books and continue to capture attention. No matter what time of year you travel to Paris, these are a few of the places that you should most definitely sprinkle into your agenda if for nothing more than to say, "I was once there."

# The Eiffel Tower

*Champ de Mars, 5 Avenue Anatole France, 75007 Paris, France*

There's not a postcard, billboard or advertisement worldwide this magnificent feat of architecture hasn't graced, and now it's yours for the trying. Construction began in 1887 under the direction of Gustave Eiffel in what was to be an impressive presentation at the 1889 World's Fair in Paris. Who could have known then that the tower would become a household name and inevitable icon of Paris.

Stretching 1,063 feet into the sky from base to cloud grazing summit, the Eiffel Tower has an uncanny way of captivating imaginations as it commands the skyline of the 7th arrondissement. Framed by Trocadéro on one end and École Militaire and the Champs de Mars on the other, it's a picturesque testament to Parisian culture. Equally charming, disarming and innovative, the tower is a marvel of latticework iron complete with three floors and a summit experience for those without aversion to great heights.

It is not a site of solitude. In fact, it's difficult to find a time of day where there isn't a line of tourists waiting to take their turn either riding the elevators up to the top floor or taking their chances with the stairs that are readily available and waiting for the climb to the second floor. The Eiffel Tower plays host to nearly 7 million visitors annually and in light of its continued international popularity, is a constant place of lively excitement. Complete with a restaurant, stunning views of the city from several levels as well as an opportunity to peek into Monsieur Eiffel's personal apartment, the tower is more than a climb—it's an experience to behold.

Perhaps even more incredible is the Eiffel Tower's ability to impress both up close and from a distance. As dusk falls over the city, it's important to gaze towards the tower on the hour as you're guaranteed to be delighted by a sparkling show of glittering lights that lasts for 5 minutes at a time. No matter how many times you witness it, there's something about the twinkling tower that's impressive and awe-inspiring. In so many ways it's fitting that the icon of Paris would capture her audience's attention time and again through lights.

# Arc de Triomphe

*Place Charles de Gaulle, 75008 Paris, France*

Follow the Champs Élysées to the west and you're guaranteed to encounter one of the most stunning sites Paris provides visitors and inhabitants alike. Rising into the sky as the centerpiece of the bustling Place Charles de Gaulle, the arch is unapologetically bold and enchanting. Construction began in 1806 by Napoleon who was looking for yet another eternal symbol of personal military success. It wasn't until 1836 that the arch was finished, and today, it's officially dedicated to the military might of France.

A walk around the arch reveals intricate stonework and impressive reliefs depicting armed glory. Visitors can easily access the urban island the arch sits on through an underground passage that directs you to either visit the base of the arch or buy a ticket to scale to the top through a series of internal stairs. While the view from above is breathtaking, below, the homage to those who have fought for France is made complete with the tomb of the unknown soldier. Buried under the arch in 1921, the grave stands for all of those who were lost fighting for the country and the flame that burns is continually fed so as to never extinguish.

The Arc de Triomphe is a thrilling tourist experience, but it's also a landmark that is called upon for important political events and is often featured in coverage of the Tour de France as cyclists make their way towards the impressive roundabout.

# Champs Élysées

*Av. des Champs-Élysées, 75008 Paris, France*

Stretched leisurely between Place de la Concorde and Place Charles de Gaulle, lies just over a mile of avenue brimming with consumer goods, food and luxury. The Champs-Élysées, celebrated famously in song and visited by thousands of people each year, is a center of consumerism and fine dining that is hard to beat. Constantly bustling from end to end, this iconic avenue hosts well-known establishments such as legendary brasserie Fouquet's, alongside recognizable shopping stops such as BMW, Abercrombie and Fitch, Sephora and Zara.

From high class to moderately priced, the avenue is interesting in the variety of consumer options it offers up. If you're searching for something extravagant to bring back home, you need look no further than the glittering Louis Vuitton Champs-Élysées location complete with silvery façade, neon lights and an open door with concierge at attention awaiting your arrival.

If your sweet tooth kicks in somewhere during your travels through the crowd, La Durée is a succulent and easily accessible solution, continuously offering up some of France's finest macarons to please the pallet. The tantalizing display of treats is hard to miss behind the warm, teal storefront that welcomes visitors in for a savory moment. With diverse stores dotting every inch of the avenue, from shops that specifically provide Parisian soccer attire to shining top-of-the line automobile displays, there's a little something to please everyone on the Champs-Élysées.

# Cathédrale Notre-Dame de Paris

*6 Parvis Notre-Dame - Pl. Jean-Paul II, 75004 Paris, France*

On any given day if one were to meander the pathways along Île de la Cité which calls it's home the 4th arrondissement of Paris, you would inevitably be met with an incredible site to behold. Casting spires up into the air 226 feet, the infamous Cathedral of Notre- Dame will flawlessly take your breath away. It is worth visiting in the name of longevity as well as the experience of wondering at such a timeless masterpiece.

What was originally begun in 1163 is today still a mesmerizing point for Parisians and visitors alike as it stuns with its meticulous gothic architecture, complete with fierce spires, looming bell towers that sound on the hour, sprawling flying buttresses and those iconic gargoyles that have inspired stage and song along the way. There is much to be admired about this cathedral, both from an outside and inside view. As you approach the main entrance, take a moment to notice the intricate stone relief work that adorns the arches above the doorway. Each arch holds its own biblical message etched in stone and statue. Make your way around the back side of the cathedral and you'll be pleasantly surprised to find yourself in the heart of a blooming garden of flowers and greenery. Built with a view in mind, it's a colorful stop overlooking the Seine that offers up a point of reflection cozied up just next to the most iconic cathedral in the world.

The interior of Notre-Dame de Paris is equally engaging and utterly spectacular to be a part of, if only for a few hours. The spacious grandeur of the cathedral alone is an overwhelming encounter from start to finish. From commanding stone columns to vast and airy heights crafted seamlessly with decorative and vaulted beams, it's a space that compels you to glance towards the heavens. A latticework of impressive colored glass makes up the beautiful rose windows that allow for pale beams of light to enter the otherwise silent sanctuary.

Visitors are invited to make their way around the interior of the cathedral unhindered. Several alcoves displaying a variety of biblical statues await and the lighting of a prayer candle at one or many is always welcome. Notre-Dame de Paris holds regular mass and the services continue both with and without visitor entrances. With several centuries at its back, and an almost mythical aura that still intrigues thousands of visitors a year, Notre-Dame de Paris is a Parisian landmark that never fails to create the wonder it promises by reputation.

# La Conciergerie

### *2 Boulevard du Palais, 75001 Paris, France*

Rising from the west of Île de la Cité is a vast and sprawling building known as the Conciergerie, with a dark history that resides behind an exquisite façade. White washed stone walls round out into a number of charming towers with coned spires crawling towards the sky. For all intents and purposes, it is intriguing in both it's immense stature and stunning aesthetic appeal. Impressive and imposing, it makes an unmistakable mark on this historic area of Paris.

However, to look a bit closer at the Conciergerie is to understand that sometimes those infamous architectural transformations that Paris is so fond of, happened under the guise of a much darker past. Gothic in architectural origin, the Conciergerie comes with all of the intriguing trappings of a building crafted to enthrall the masses. It was within those same walls, that many souls awaited their fate in the past. What was once the Capetian seat of power in the 10th century slipped into role of prison during the course of the French revolution. Hundreds of individuals were held at the Conciergerie as they awaited their turn at the guillotine. One such individual included the infamous Marie Antoinette.

When the bloodshed of the French revolution finally ceased, the Conciergerie continued its tradition as a high-profile prison through the 19th century. It underwent drastic reconstruction only towards the end of the century and in 1914 was eventually redesigned and designated as a national monument.

Today, the Conciergerie is available for tours, but is limited in public access points. The majority of the structure is dedicated to French courts of law. Even so, a walk by the Conciergerie is an exercise in acknowledgment of those who once upon a time, waited within its solid walls only to meet their tragic fate elsewhere in the city. It is a place that stands out of time with the memory of thousands upon thousands of stories and lives.

Rising into the Parisian sky, dominating the west bank of the Île de la Cité, the Conciergerie is still a testament to a bitter story that remains intact within the very wall. It is worth a moment of memory and reflection during your time in Paris.

# Chapter 19: Last Minute Tips and Tricks

Whether you've been dreaming of visiting Paris your entire existence, or you travel to the City of Light multiple times a year, it never hurts to consider a few tips and tricks that could potentially make the experience a bit smoother all the way around.

## Taking Control of the Tourist Ticket Situation

You are absolutely certain you want to see a number of major monuments during your trip, but one thing that is hard to work around for even the most seasoned traveler, especially during high tourism season, is a long line. From the Arc de Triomphe to the Eiffel Tower, the winding queue resulting from thousands of passionate tourists from around the world is almost inevitable.

As a strategy to avoiding the wait time, consider buying tickets for yourself and those you are traveling with online ahead of time. Websites dedicated to these major Parisian icons are available in a variety of languages and provide the opportunity to have a ticket in hand when you arrive. This route allows you to successfully jump the line and manages to save you a lot of stress in the meantime.

Another thing to consider when traveling to Paris is the one thing nobody in the world can control, no matter how hard we may try, and that's the weather. Paris is a city that tends to fluctuate on the weather-front. What is forecast as a completely sunny, cloudless afternoon in July could prove itself to be an experience in torrential rainfall by noon. Luckily, these outbursts from above don't tend to last long, but they can most definitely affect your plans for visiting those infamous monuments.

If you're budget allows for it, it's never a bad idea to purchase two sets of tickets for those important visits that mean the most to you. Having separate sets of tickets for two different times of the day, or even two separate days during the week will help ensure that a turn of the weather doesn't affect your ability to see that site you've had your heart set on for so long.

## Making the Most of the Metro

The beauty of making your way around Paris by underground transportation is that it's extremely easy to maneuver. With a metro system that seamlessly links all major neighborhoods and tends to be timely, you'll find it's a quick and efficient way to get from point A to point B in Paris, and fairly painless to navigate altogether. One thing that might not be as clear is what the best way is to prepare yourself with tickets. Each metro station hosts several kiosks where tickets can be purchased. Additionally, there are nearly always transportation staff available who can sell you tickets directly at the window. While there are plenty of choices when it comes to tickets, the sheer number of options is exactly what can make it confusing.

If you're going to be visiting Paris for a week, it's worth your time to purchase the week pass through the digital kiosk. This saves you time and reduces the hassle of having to cart around multiple tickets that are easily lost in pockets or on the wind as you move from one station to the next. This week- long ticket gives you access to the major zones of Paris and is a singular item to keep track of as you travel. If you are only going to be in Paris for a few days, daily passes are also available for anywhere between 1-4 days of visiting.

In the event you are only planning on taking the metro a limited number of times, but want to save on cost, purchasing a book of 10 tickets is your most financially efficient option. Finally, if you're planning on visiting Paris long-term, it's always good to consider an investment in a Navigo pass. Rechargeable on a monthly basis by digital kiosk at the station or online, a Navigo allows frequent metro travelers to save money and simply swipe their cards at the turnstile for access.

Do note you will have to send in an official application to obtain this pass, and each card requires a photo as well as a long-term residence in France. Photo booths are located in nearly every major metro station to remind you to smile for the camera once you receive your card. A Navigo discovered without a photo is likely to come with a fee from a transportation official.

# Chapter 20: À Bientôt- See You soon!

Whether you are reading this because you stumbled across it on a regular day of living life, or you've turned to it prior to a long-planned trip to France or even possibly after you've already travelled to Paris, it's of the upmost importance to remember that a travel guide is nothing more or less than the very beginning of your story. It is my opinion that Paris is an endless tale to be told, complete with all the twists and plot turns that make any great story worth following. With a history seeped in drama, flavor, art and romance, it's not hard to figure out why people from across the planet continue to trek towards this city of intrigue in the hopes of experiencing that certain something Paris possesses that sets it apart from the rest.

The following piece of advice is equally directed at those travelers who plan meticulously as well as those who fly along on whimsy alone: Paris is a city to be walked.

If you do nothing else during your time in this remarkable place, make sure your steps outnumber your travel time by car, taxi or metro. It is a city worth walking purely in light of the fact that the best and most unexpected moments you'll encounter will inevitably be as you wander aimlessly along. This might sound strange, but it's entirely true. As you meander the banks of the Seine, there's no telling what fantastic scene you might stumble upon. Turn a random corner and you could be met with the resonating song of nuns flowing out of the door of an unknown cathedral you previously missed on the map. Circle around the Montparnasse Tower and you could be surprised by the impromptu clang and clatter, complete with horns and sirens as transportation workers strike for their rights and claim the grandest boulevards as their own for the day. If you're walking at twilight, you could find yourself the centerpiece of Seine side tango, caught up in a wave of music and movement unexpectedly.

Great cities are equal parts past, present and the people they possess. Between the stunning architecture, deeply moving history, flavorful food and the colorful combination of fashion and film, Paris is a city full of people seeking inspiration and living lives made to intersect. Travel becomes the most interesting when you start to realize where the lines of similarity and difference lie. Blending those lines is the goal and as you meet and mingle with the people of Paris, whoever they may be, it's inevitable that you'll return home a bit better for it. It's exciting to consider the impact you may leave on the city and its unsuspecting inhabitants just as equally as they will undoubtedly leave an impression on you. In this way, travel is always a valuable two- way street.

As you've read through this book of Parisian inspiration, because ultimately, that's what it's always been meant to be, I hope that your imagination has started to turn wildly. It would be thrilling to think that upon the closing of any chapter, a reader would begin furiously making notes of their own on whatever scrap of paper is easily accessible. These notes may be comparisons between the Paris you've experienced for yourself to the one I've described here.  They may simply be thoughts and notes of excitement and potential as you consider the unknown and perhaps begin imagining yourself in a city where so many others have fallen in love before you.

Whatever direction your thoughts go, I hope they are Paris-bound and end up with a trip overseas in the near future. If you do find yourself on a flight bound for Charles de Gaulle airport anytime soon, I would encourage you to bring a copy of this along. Simply stuff it in your suitcase in place of those previously mentioned expectations and be on your way. In the spirit of travel, feel free to use its pages to keep track of your own time abroad and if all goes well, you'll have several new locations to add as you explore.

This is your jumping off point, and the hope is that there is much more to see and do than you could have ever imagined once you land in France. Your travels are as alive and growing as Paris itself. As you add your own history to the city just by being there, you'll find a place all your own. Paris is waiting for you—so what are you waiting for?

# About the Expert

Caitlyn Knuth is a lifelong writer who was inspired to put a pen to paper as a child long before spelling skills were acquired. Constantly captivated by the pictures words alone have the power to paint, and the owner of a spirit that is always ready for the next travel adventure, she's found her muse alive and well in the city of Paris, France.

After several years spent studying and working in the City of Light and eventually returning home, she realized that no matter how far she went, Paris was always there in the back of her mind, demanding to be acknowledged, in the chicest way possible of course.

So...she gave in to the call of the city once again and began writing about her own experiences in France. Through these recollections and personal points of insight, she hopes to reach those who feel Paris inspiring them from a distance and help them find the courage to set off on their own adventures in the City of Love and Light.

HowExpert publishes quick 'how to' guides on all topics from A to Z by everyday experts. Visit HowExpert.com to learn more.

# Recommended Resources

- HowExpert.com – Quick 'How To' Guides on All Topics from A to Z by Everyday Experts.
- HowExpert.com/free – Free HowExpert Email Newsletter.
- HowExpert.com/books – HowExpert Books
- HowExpert.com/courses – HowExpert Courses
- HowExpert.com/clothing – HowExpert Clothing
- HowExpert.com/membership – HowExpert Membership Site
- HowExpert.com/affiliates – HowExpert Affiliate Program
- HowExpert.com/writers – Write About Your #1 Passion/Knowledge/Expertise & Become a HowExpert Author.
- HowExpert.com/resources – Additional HowExpert Recommended Resources
- YouTube.com/HowExpert – Subscribe to HowExpert YouTube.
- Instagram.com/HowExpert – Follow HowExpert on Instagram.
- Facebook.com/HowExpert – Follow HowExpert on Facebook.

CPSIA information can be obtained
at www.ICGtesting.com
Printed in the USA
BVHW061109170223
658731BV00002B/242